HAPPY
COOKING!

Deborah

ENTERTAINING
made easy with *Deborah Hutton*

ENTERTAINING
made easy with *Deborah Hutton*

Contents

Welcome

I LOVE NOTHING MORE than getting together with good friends, setting the table, chilling the drinks and cooking up a storm at home. Sharing meals with family and friends plays an important role in creating a sense of belonging. It's important to stay connected, nurture our relationships and spend quality time in a relaxed environment. While it's fun to eat out and try new places, there's something very special about having people over for a home-cooked meal.

I hear people say, "I don't have the time" or "I can't cook and it's too hard", but this guide is guaranteed to make at-home entertaining easy. Whether it's a casual lunch, a formal dinner party or a sumptuous banquet, you'll be able to show off your entertaining skills and impress your guests with the practical tips and delicious recipes that follow.

This book provides simple advice on hosting fabulous occasions with minimal fuss and maximum enjoyment. You'll find plenty of information on how to plan your next event and serve mouth-watering recipes your guests will love.

There's also practical advice on menus and decorations. We've covered it all – from invitations, settings, appetisers and welcome drinks through to main courses and desserts. You'll find everything you need to plan and pull off memorable get-togethers.

Opening your home to friends and family is enriching and fun, so get creative and join me in reigniting the culture of entertaining at home.

Deborah

THE ESSENCE OF
Entertai

Entertaining at home allows us to connect with friends and family on a more intimate level, and also welcome new friends. It's a great way to share experiences, let your guard down and relax over a glass of champagne.

Entertaining is all about good food and wine, good friends and good fun. The goal of successful entertaining isn't so much about impressing people, but putting them at ease and having a few laughs.

LUNCHES

Daytime entertaining is more relaxed. I adore a lazy Sunday lunch with plenty of time to prepare in the morning. But if everyone's having a good time, it can lead into early evening, so be warned!

Dinner parties

THEY CAN RANGE FROM HAVING FRIENDS OVER FOR A CASUAL "CHOP" TO FULLY CATERED THREE-COURSE FEASTS.

Cocktail parties

What a great way to have more people over at once for some seriously good fun! I love creating an interesting mix of guests and just letting the conversation and drinks flow. Food can be as easy as chicken sandwiches, or as sophisticated as canapés. Make sure you have plenty of drinks on hand – a dry cocktail party is one your friends will never let you forget!

WHEN DISASTER STRIKES... A few of my mishaps have turned out to be the funniest occasions ever. Once I found myself trying to salvage a chocolate panettone pudding I'd dropped on my stone floor in front of eight horrified guests! Next thing, I was on my knees trying to find anything edible. Thankfully, the wine was flowing... Soon I had three friends on the floor with me, in fits of laughter, also looking for panettone chunks we could eat.

Entertaining
ESSENTIALS

There must be some hidden alchemy,
a lively cocktail of personalities and
a sense of occasion. The key is
all about you and your guests
enjoying one another's company, with
delicious food and a setting that
creates a little anticipation.

FRIENDS

It's important to create a great guest list. Think about a good mix of interesting, like-minded people, with a few "funsters" thrown in for good measure – you need one or two strong personalities to help keep the conversation flowing while you're engaged in the kitchen. Entertaining is about your guests having fun, engaging in good conversations and meeting new people.

Be prepared

I like to be organised, have the table set, arrival drinks ready and the music on so I can concentrate on welcoming guests. Successful entertaining comes down to proper preparation, which allows the host to relax and focus on spending time with his or her guests.

Good food

IT DOESN'T HAVE TO BE THREE COURSES OR OVERLY FANCY, AND YOU DON'T NEED TO BE A MASTER CHEF! IF YOU CAN'T COOK, THEN YOU CAN ALWAYS SERVE UP YOUR FAVOURITE TAKEAWAY ON A PERFECTLY SET TABLE!

ANYONE CAN DO IT

You don't need years of experience or a large budget to entertain guests at your place. Some of my most successful events have been the simplest. If you don't consider yourself a good cook, I've included some easy no-fail recipes that will help build your confidence. Think about the setting: buy yourself some decent plates, cloth napkins and good wine glasses. Make the table the centrepiece, with fresh flowers, candles or small interesting objects from around the home.

"Good etiquette is about hosts and their guests doing the right thing by each other and creating a comfortable experience, from invitations through to the goodbyes."

DON'T BE LATE

Guests should show up on time and hosts can never be late for their own party. If a guest is late, don't hold up the food for more than half an hour. Late arrivals shouldn't expect everyone to wait. Also, if you're planning a late or noisy night, think about inviting your neighbours or letting them know.

Welcoming guests

ALWAYS GREET YOUR GUESTS AT THE DOOR WITH A BIG SMILE AND A WELCOME DRINK. MAKE SURE YOU PROPERLY INTRODUCE EVERYONE.

The key objective is to have your guests relax and enjoy themselves.

The perfect host

DON'T LOCK YOURSELF IN THE KITCHEN AT THE EXPENSE OF HAVING FUN WITH YOUR GUESTS. AT THE DINING TABLE, ENSURE EVERYONE IS INCLUDED IN THE CONVERSATION.

After dessert

Try not to clear the table too quickly. Let people linger and the conversation flow. A change of scenery can be a nice gear change, so think about offering coffee or a drink in another room.

Getting

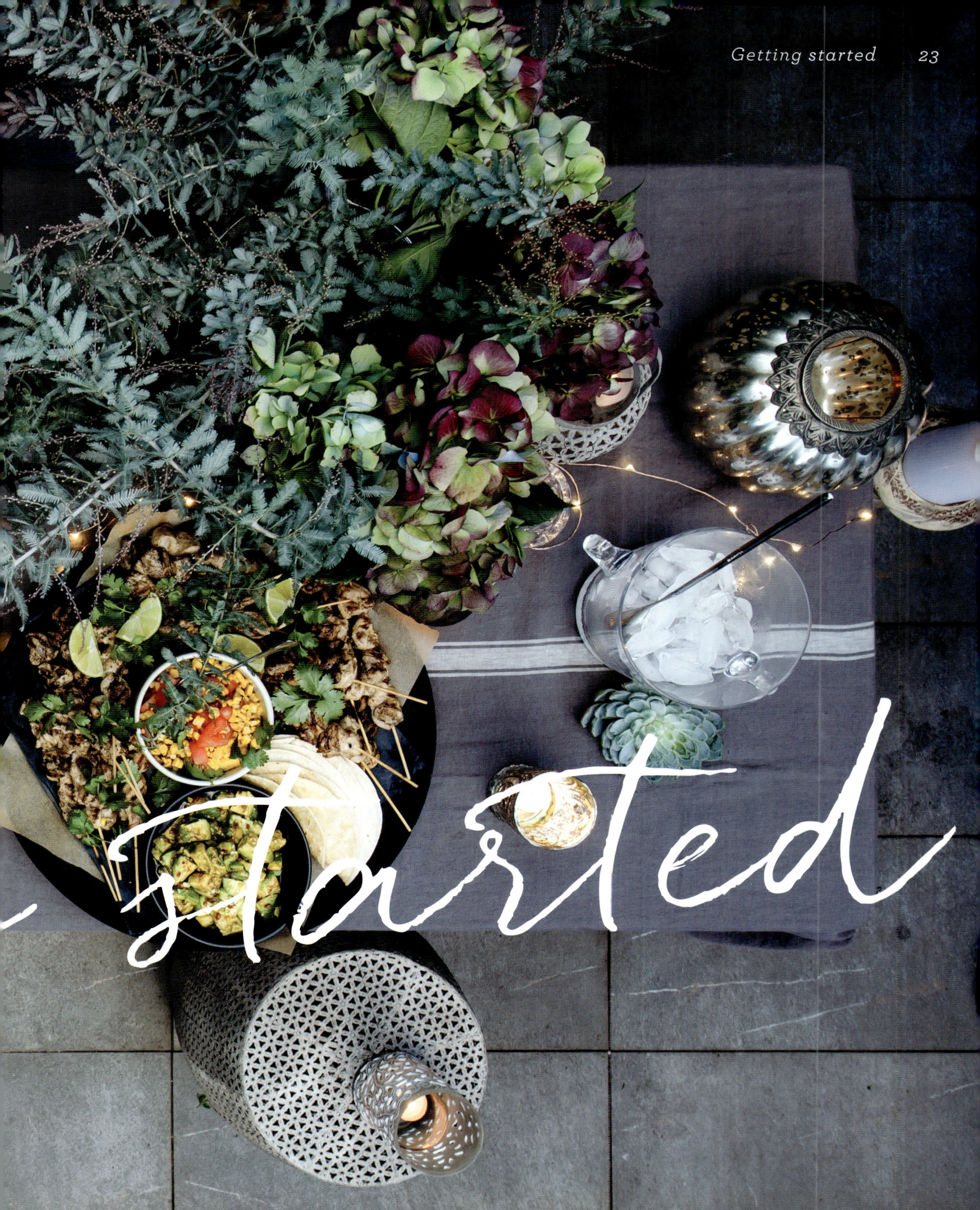

"A little preparation goes a long way to creating a wonderful experience for your guests and helping your occasion run smoothly from beginning to end. Here are some key points to consider when planning to entertain."

THE OCCASION

It's important to consider the occasion, as this will help you come up with a menu, drinks list, decorations and even a theme for your party. Are you planning a laid-back lunch to catch up with family and friends, or a decadent cocktail party to celebrate a birthday? The occasion will determine the look and feel of your party.

Guests

MY DINING TABLE SITS EIGHT, PERFECT FOR CONVERSATIONS. I TRY TO INVITE PEOPLE WITH COMMON INTERESTS FROM DIFFERENT WALKS OF LIFE, AND I LIKE TO MIX THINGS UP WITH A VARIETY OF PERSONALITIES, INCLUDING A FEW WHO ARE LARGER THAN LIFE TO SPARK CONVERSATION.

Menu

Plan your menu well in advance. I like to serve up light, fresh foods in summer, and hearty, slow-cooked meals in cooler months. Try to source fresh seasonal produce and let the food speak for itself.

Drinks

Once you've finalised the menu, think about which wines might complement the food. When guests arrive, be sure to offer them a drink. Have plenty of ice on hand, and also enough serving glasses.

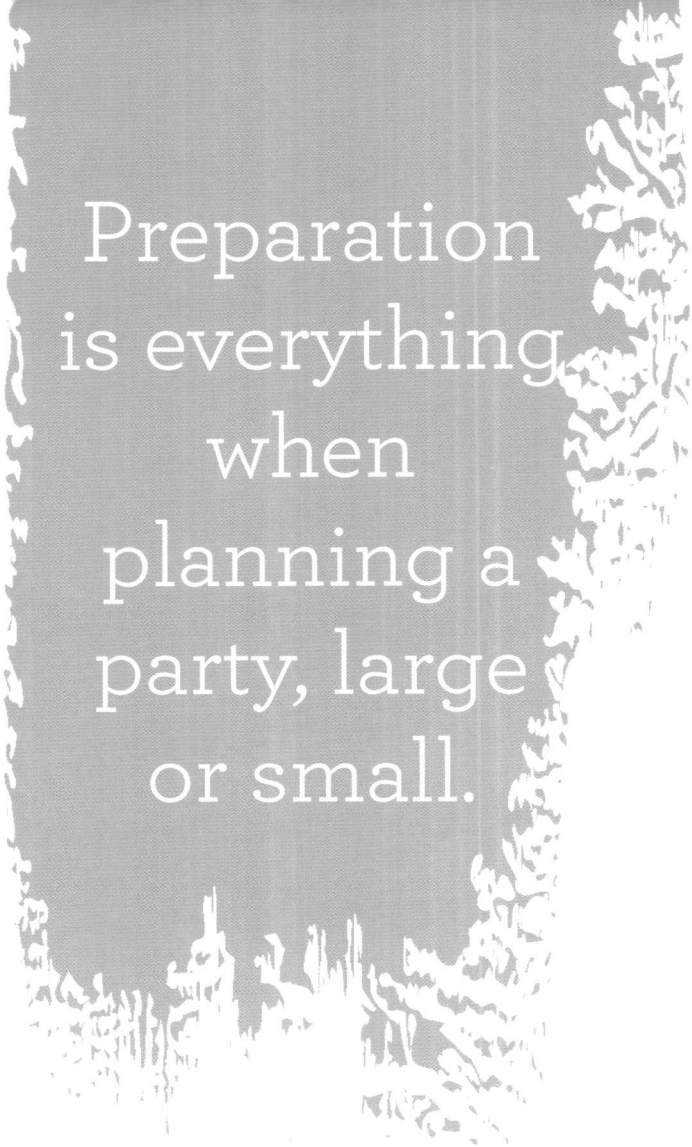

Preparation is everything when planning a party, large or small.

Budget

SET A BUDGET FOR FOOD, DRINKS, TABLEWARE AND DECORATIONS. IF YOUR BUDGET IS TIGHT, CONSIDER A "POTLUCK" OR BYO OCCASION.

Food shopping

Buy items like drinks and dry goods well in advance, and perishable items in the days leading up to your occasion. Avoid a budget blowout by good planning.

MUSIC

Music is central to creating the right ambience. It should be relaxing when guests arrive, perhaps picking up tempo towards the end of the meal, and be more uplifting after you've eaten. To free up time for cooking and mingling, it really helps to have prepared playlists that will play continuously from when guests arrive until they leave. I usually have a good idea of the sort of music I want to play and start compiling playlists in the lead-up.

In the mood

CREATING A SENSE OF OCCASION CAN BE JUST AS IMPORTANT AS THE FOOD AND DRINKS. I LIKE TO THINK ABOUT THE ROOM AS A WHOLE, WITH THE DINING TABLE AS THE CENTREPIECE AND COORDINATED DECOR.

Themes

Add extra fun to your event by choosing a theme, which doesn't have to be expensive or time-consuming. It can be as low-key or as imaginative as you like, from an alfresco lunch to sophisticated cocktails. See pages 98-105 for some ideas.

INVITATIONS

I call or email friends a few weeks – sometimes months – in advance to check their availability. I start with people who are central to an occasion (like the birthday guest), to coordinate dates, and then invite other guests when the date is confirmed. Once you get people locked in, follow up with an email. If you don't hear from someone, follow up with a phone call. Be sure to get confirmed responses and then send a "looking forward to seeing you" email a few days before your occasion. If it's a special event, it's nice to follow up with a written invitation. A little formality can create a great sense of anticipation.

Relax

PERFECTION IS OVERRATED! GUESTS WILL BE THRILLED TO BE GIVEN A HOME-COOKED MEAL. ALL THAT REALLY MATTERS IS THAT YOU ENJOY YOURSELF.

YOUR INVITATION SHOULD INCLUDE

DATE AND TIME: Be specific about the time you want your guests to arrive. For example, 6:30pm for a 7pm dinner.

LOCATION: Include your address and directions, or a map if your place is difficult to find, and info on where to park.

RSVP: Include an RSVP request with your phone number and email address.

OCCASION: Let your guests know what the occasion is, particularly if it's someone's birthday. If you have a theme in mind, make sure your invitation reflects that.

DRESS: Let guests know if it's a casual barbecue or a formal dinner, and include a dress code, whether it's "jeans", "smart casual" or "cocktail".

THE Menu

The menu plays a starring role and every meal begins with a flash of inspiration – an inkling of a flavour or a mood you'd like to create.

PLANNING

Be realistic about the space you have to work with and the amount of fuss you want to make. When thinking about the menu, consider your cooking experience, budget and the dietary needs of your guests. Also keep in mind the season and availability of quality produce. So I can spend more time with my guests, I prefer recipes that I'm familiar with and where the bulk of preparation can be done in advance, then to reheat closer to serving time. Wash, chop and blanch ingredients well beforehand and keep them under wraps in the fridge until you're ready to mix and serve. In winter, I like slow oven-cooked dishes that can be finished earlier and kept warm until guests arrive. This helps free up time to prepare drinks and side dishes. If you have a small oven, use recipes that can be pre-prepared or cooked on the stove, instead of multiple oven recipes that require cooking at various times and temperatures. I always warm up plates before serving hot dishes. With cold appetisers, make them ahead and keep them wrapped and refrigerated until serving time.

Appetisers

TO SET THE MOOD AND KEEP THINGS CASUAL, IT'S A LOVELY SIGHT FOR GUESTS TO WALK IN AND SEE AN OPEN PLATTER OF DELICIOUS DELICACIES, SOMETHING THAT TEASES THE PALATE, SETS A GOOD FIRST IMPRESSION AND IS EASY TO PREPARE BEFORE EVERYONE ARRIVES.

ENTRÉES

Entrées are the prelude to the main course, so they should both tantalise and excite but not overload. Keep the selection simple, as you don't want to have your kitchen overrun by just serving the first course! Entrées encompass soups, salads and any other starters that you can prep well beforehand. My repertoire includes risotto, gnocchi, ravioli and serves of succulent seafood.

LAST-MINUTE TAKEAWAY MEALS

It's good to have last-minute recipes that you can pull together out of the fridge just in case things go wrong in the kitchen, or if extra guests drop in unexpectedly. Check online for places that deliver good food in your area: local takeaways, great delis and supermarkets with pre-prepared mains and desserts. Presentation is key, so make sure to serve everything in beautiful dishes, adding freshly chopped herbs for a lovely finishing touch.

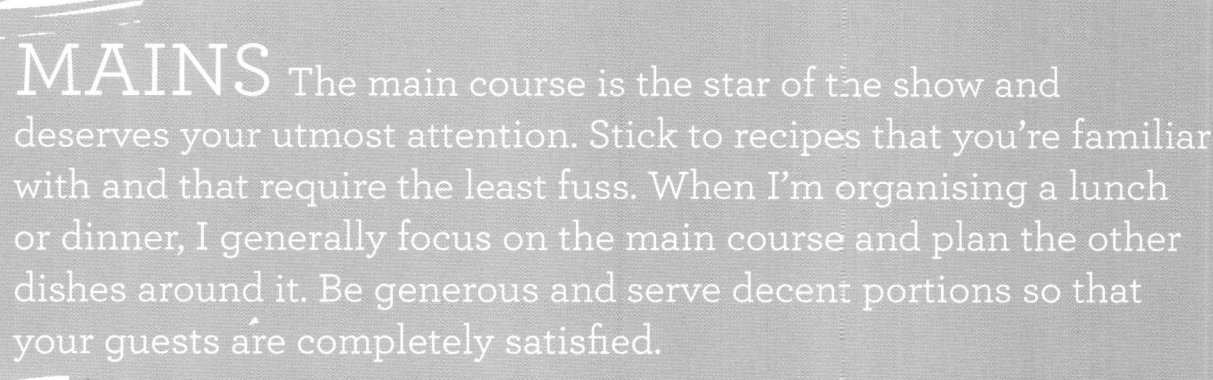

MAINS

The main course is the star of the show and deserves your utmost attention. Stick to recipes that you're familiar with and that require the least fuss. When I'm organising a lunch or dinner, I generally focus on the main course and plan the other dishes around it. Be generous and serve decent portions so that your guests are completely satisfied.

DESSERTS

An amazing dessert leaves a lasting impression and, if all else fails, can rescue an average dinner. Think about serving a combination of decadent and healthy desserts so all guests are catered for. Play around with recipes until you have some fabulous no-fail desserts. If you don't have time to prepare something, there are lots of other options, such as bowls of chocolate and gelato, or hit the patisseries that sell delicious cakes and tarts.

Emergency snacks

YOU'RE RUNNING LATE AND GUESTS ARE ARRIVING! TAKE A BREATH AND REACH FOR EMERGENCY SNACKS: OLIVES, CRACKERS, CHEESES, PISTACHIOS, ALMONDS, POPCORN, SAVOURY CHIPS AND GOOD DELI DIPS. PRESENTATION MAKES ALL THE DIFFERENCE, SO SHOW THEM OFF IN LOVELY SERVING DISHES.

TO-DO *List*

Get ready well before your occasion and allow plenty of time for contingencies. When I'm well prepared, everything runs much more smoothly and I have a better time with less effort.

A simple to-do list for an informal barbecue might be something like this:

☐ confirm arrival time

☐ shop for ingredients

☐ chill drinks

☐ get plenty of ice

☐ check the gas bottle

For more elaborate occasions, you might like to use a checklist like the one at right, which can be customised to your needs. Tick it off as you go and take it with you while you're shopping.

TWO WEEKS BEFORE

☐ Check RSVPs
☐ Finalise menu; double-check dietary requirements

ONE WEEK BEFORE

☐ Shop for, or order online, grocery items, drinks and decorations
☐ Compile your favourite tunes for the music playlist

THE DAY BEFORE

☐ Double-check final ingredients and drinks
☐ Buy fresh ingredients and fresh flowers
☐ Marinate and prepare recipes ahead, where possible
☐ Tidy up lounge, dining room and bathroom, and add fresh hand towels

ON THE DAY

☐ Set table; select serving dishes
☐ Decorate, if there's a particular theme
☐ Buy ice and chill drinks
☐ Prepare and cook what you can in advance
☐ Have drinks and starters ready when guests arrive
☐ Leave at least half an hour to get ready

MARTINI
(recipe on page 43)

THE Cocktail Party

There's always a thrill of anticipation when you're offered a chilled cocktail on arrival.

Drinks
ESSENTIALS

Successful entertaining is all about creating the perfect atmosphere for guests to relax and enjoy themselves. An important part of this is planning the drinks menu, as an essential element of good entertaining is getting the mix of drinks right. The most important thing, though, is have your drinks chilled and ready when the doorbell rings.

ARRIVAL DRINKS

Consider welcoming guests with a refreshing cocktail in a beautiful glass. Champagnes and sparkling wines should be served cold, so make sure they're well chilled before serving and that they remain that way. An ice bucket comes in handy, especially in the warmer months. If you're having a themed occasion, a specific region or era, this may influence your drinks menu. However, arrival drinks don't have to match the food, as they're more about setting the scene and making it festive. Remember that some guests may prefer non-alcoholic drinks, so stock up on sparkling mineral water, soft drinks, juices and jugs of water with slices of fresh lemon and lime.

The Bar

A DO-IT-YOURSELF COCKTAIL BAR CAN ADD A SENSE OF FUN AND FREE UP YOUR TIME FOR COOKING. YOU CAN SET UP A MODIFIED BAR WITH A HANDFUL OF WINES AND BEERS (ESPECIALLY IN SUMMER) AND MIXERS ON ICE. BAR STAPLES INCLUDE VODKA, VERMOUTH, GIN, LEMONS, LIMES, MARTINI OLIVES, TONIC WATER AND SODA WATER. DON'T FORGET TO INCLUDE SOME LIGHT BEERS AS WELL.

GLASSWARE

Try to serve wines in the correct wine glasses, where possible, such as goblets for red wines. You'll also need a decanter, to let mature wine breathe, and a large ice bucket to keep your white wines chilled. Be sure to have matching sets of champagne glasses, tall highballs, martini glasses and tumblers for short drinks and spirits. Large jugs are great for serving water, cocktails and sangria.

Drinks

REDS

Red wines are more enjoyable served at room temperature. Try my menu matches.

CABERNET SAUVIGNON

Taste: Concentrated and lush with layers of flavour like black currant, blackberry and cedar. **Goes with:** Beef, lamb and burgers.

MERLOT

Taste: Soft, fruity, velvety and intense, with plum and dark berry flavours. **Goes with:** Roast lamb, lamb chops and duck.

PINOT NOIR

Taste: Silky texture, restrained fruit and earthy. **Goes with:** Beef, ribs, veal, lamb, pork and salmon.

SHIRAZ

Taste: Full bodied with firm acidity and flavours of wild herbs and Asian spices. **Goes with:** Beef, lamb and game.

WHITES

Crisp white wines are best served chilled. Try my menu matches.

RIESLING

Taste: Crisp and refreshing with notes of apple and citrus. **Goes with:** Spicy and fusion foods, Japanese and smoked salmon.

SAUVIGNON BLANC

Taste: Grassy, fruity and herbal with mineral character. **Goes with:** Seafood, light pastas and goat's cheese.

PINOT GRIS

Taste: Fresh, fragrant, rich and full-bodied with flavours of spiced apple. **Goes with:** Delicate seafood, tuna, pork and Asian dishes.

CHARDONNAY

Taste: Ranges in style from crisp to full-bodied oak. **Goes with:** Salmon, tuna, seafood risotto and roast chicken.

COCKTAILS add some sparkle to your occasions. When choosing cocktails, think about the season and theme of your event. Mojitos and margaritas are refreshing in summer, while rum-based drinks and mulled wines are good winter warmers. Some cocktails can be mixed ahead of time and served in jugs with ice when guests arrive.

BARWARE ESSENTIALS FOR MIXING IN STYLE

BOTTLE OPENER
The most essential bar gadget... bar none!

SHAKER
The key to well-mixed cocktails. Choose one with a strainer.

SHOT GLASSES
Good for post-dinner shots and pouring accurate quantities.

GOOD-SIZED JUG
For serving cocktails, sodas and juices.

BLENDER
For mixing cocktails and juices. Pick one with enough power to crush ice.

ICE BUCKET
Have ice close on hand for cocktails and keeping bottles chilled.

DECORATIONS
Add some fun to your cocktails with swizzle sticks, umbrellas, straws and lemongrass.

MARTINI

"I was first seduced into drinking dry martinis when James Bond reached for his 'shaken not stirred'! It packs a punch and should be consumed as dry as possible, with just a hint of the vermouth. I personally prefer it with a green olive, but a ribbon of lemon rind works just as well."

Ingredients

60ml dry vermouth
½ cup ice-cubes
60ml good-quality vodka, chilled
1 sicilian green olive, rinsed

Method

1 Pour 1 tablespoon of the vermouth into a chilled martini glass. Swirl vermouth around the glass to coat the side.
2 Place the ice-cubes in a chilled cocktail shaker. Add the vodka and the remaining vermouth and shake for 1 minute or until well combined.
3 Strain the vodka into the glass. Skewer the olive on a toothpick and add to glass. Serve immediately.

BARBADOS

SERVES	PREP + COOK TIME
12	25 MINUTES

Ingredients

8 passionfruit

1½ cups (330g) caster sugar

1 cup (250ml) water

1 pineapple (1.2kg), peeled, halved, sliced thinly

4 medium oranges (960g)

1 cup (250ml) dark underproof rum, chilled

2 cups (500ml) lemonade, chilled

crushed ice, to serve

Method

1 Remove the pulp from passionfruit; reserve.

2 Place the sugar in a large heavy-based frying pan over medium heat; cook, stirring, until a dark caramel colour (the sugar will start to dissolve, then form clumps; as you continue to stir, it will eventually liquefy).

3 Carefully add the water and passionfruit pulp to the sugar (the mixture will spit); when the bubbles subside, stir the mixture until smooth. Pour mixture into a large stainless steel bowl, add pineapple; turn to coat in mixture.

4 Cut 1 orange into slices; juice the remaining oranges. Add orange juice and orange slices to the bowl with the rum and lemonade; stir to combine.

5 One-third fill a jug with crushed ice. Add rum and fruit mixture; serve immediately.

TIPPLE TIP

The caramel will burn if it touches your skin, so be extra careful when adding the liquid to the melted sugar. Add the liquid down the side of the pan, not over the top, keeping your arm well out of the way of the boiling caramel.

CUCUMBER
BASIL GIMLET

SERVES	PREP TIME
10	15 MINUTES

"To turn this into a sparkling mocktail for the designated driver, simply replace the gin with a big splash of soda water."

Ingredients

1¼ cups (275g) caster sugar

1 cup firmly packed basil leaves

5 lebanese cucumbers (650g), chopped coarsely

crushed ice, to serve

700ml gin, chilled

½ cup (125ml) strained lime juice

¼ cup basil leaves, extra

1 lebanese cucumber, extra, sliced thinly lengthways into ribbons (see tip)

Method

1 Process sugar, basil and chopped cucumber in a food processor until smooth.
2 Fill a large jug one-third full with crushed ice. Strain cucumber mixture through a fine sieve into jug, pushing down on solids to extract all liquid; discard solids. Add gin and juice; stir well to combine. Serve topped with extra basil and sliced cucumber.

TIPPLE TIP

It's easy to slice the extra cucumber lengthways into ribbons by using a vegetable peeler.

MARGARITA

SERVES	PREP TIME
1	5 MINUTES

"Margaritas are a refreshing must-have cocktail for Mexican fiestas. They're a perennial favourite of mine, especially in the summer months."

Ingredients

30ml tequila

30ml cointreau

30ml fresh lime juice

½ cup ice-cubes

sea salt flakes, for rim of glass

Method

1 Pour tequila, Cointreau and lime juice over ice-cubes in a cocktail shaker; shake well.

2 Salt the rim of a chilled cocktail glass.

3 Pour the mixture with ice-cubes into glass. Garnish with lime wedges, if you like.

TEA PARTY TIPPLE

SERVES

10

PREP TIME

15 MINUTES
+ REFRIGERATION
& STANDING

Ingredients

20cm stalk lemongrass (40g)

2 earl grey tea bags

⅓ cup (75g) caster sugar

1½ cups (375ml) boiling water

ice-cubes

1 medium lemon (140g), halved lengthways, sliced thinly

2 x 300ml bottles dry ginger ale, chilled

⅓ cup (80ml) strained lemon juice

1 cup (250ml) gin

Method

1 Trim lemongrass, cut in half lengthways; place in a heatproof jug. Add tea bags, sugar and the boiling water, stir until sugar dissolves; stand for 10 minutes. Discard tea bags; cover, then refrigerate until cold.

2 To serve, one-third fill a jug with ice-cubes; add lemon slices, tea mixture with lemongrass stalks, ginger ale, lemon juice and gin. Stir to combine.

TIPPLE TIP

For a decorative element, make your own tea bags with 4 small squares of muslin and ½ teaspoon of loose tea in each; tie with string and leave in the jug to serve.

APEROL SPRITZ

SERVES

1

PREP TIME

5 MINUTES

"Originating in northern Italy, Aperol spritz has become my favourite summer drink. It's a great way to start a meal and whet the appetite."

Ingredients

90ml prosecco (or another dry sparkling white wine)

½ cup ice-cubes

dash of soda

60ml aperol aperitif

1 slice lime or orange, to garnish

Method

1 Pour prosecco into a glass over ice-cubes.
2 Add the dash of soda and top with Aperol.
3 Gently stir with a spoon and garnish with a lime or orange slice.

PASSIONFRUIT PISCO PUNCH

SERVES

8

PREP + COOK TIME

15 MINUTES
+ COOLING
& REFRIGERATION

"Pisco is a grape brandy made in Peru and Chile that was developed by Spanish settlers way back in the 16th century. It's worth tracking down."

Ingredients

¾ cup (165g) caster sugar

¾ cup (180ml) water

¾ cup (180ml) passionfruit pulp

2 tablespoons lemon juice

1½ cups (375ml) pisco
(or white rum)

3 cups ice-cubes

3 cups (750ml) soda water

1 small lemon (120g), sliced thinly

1 passionfruit, quartered
lengthways, extra

8 large sprigs mint

Method

1 Stir sugar and the water in a small saucepan over medium heat until sugar dissolves. Bring to the boil. Remove from heat; cool. Refrigerate until cold.

2 Press the passionfruit pulp through a sieve over a small jug or bowl. Return 1 tablespoon of the seeds to the jug; discard remaining seeds.

3 Just before serving, combine 1 cup (250ml) of the sugar syrup, the passionfruit juice mixture, lemon juice, pisco and ice-cubes in a large jug. Add soda water, lemon slices and extra passionfruit wedges; stir gently. Serve topped with mint.

GREEN GRAPE & APPLE SPRITZER

SERVES

4

PREP TIME

10 MINUTES

"Delicious alcohol-free beverages
should be part of every host's repertoire.
This spritzer is the perfect example."

Ingredients

500g seedless green grapes

**1 large apple (200g),
chopped coarsely**

2 cups (500ml) soda water, chilled

1 lime, sliced thinly

Method

1 Using an electric juicer, extract juice from grapes and apple.
2 Combine juice with soda water and lime in a large serving jug.

TIPPLE TIP

Freeze some extra seedless green grapes and add to the spritzer for decoration and to help keep the drink chilled; or serve over ice.

RHUBARB & ELDERFLOWER MOJITO

SERVES
8

PREP + COOK TIME
10 MINUTES
+ COOLING

"This takes the popular mojito to a whole new level. Serve this pretty concoction in cool jam jars with some sweet strawberries."

Ingredients

300g rhubarb, cut into 10cm lengths

2 cups (440g) caster sugar

2 cups (500ml) water

¼ teaspoon ground nutmeg

1 vanilla bean, split lengthways, seeds scraped

8 limes (720g), chopped coarsely

1 cup loosely packed mint leaves

1 cup (250ml) white rum, chilled

⅓ cup (80ml) elderflower cordial

1 cup ice-cubes

1.25 litres (5 cups) soda water, chilled

Method

1 Place rhubarb, sugar, the water, nutmeg, vanilla pod and scraped seeds in a medium saucepan over medium heat, stirring until sugar dissolves. Bring to the boil. Reduce heat; simmer, uncovered, for 5 minutes. Cool.

2 Strain rhubarb mixture over a bowl; reserve syrup. Keep rhubarb for another use (see tips). Place lime and mint in a large serving jug. Crush with a muddling stick or rolling pin to release the juice. Add reserved rhubarb syrup, rum, elderflower cordial and ice-cubes. Top with soda water.

TIPPLE TIPS

You can reserve the strained rhubarb to flavour smoothies, or spoon on top of porridge, cereal or yoghurt.

The rhubarb syrup can be made up to 3 days ahead; cover and refrigerate.

MACCHITINO

SERVES	PREP TIME
10	15 MINUTES + REFRIGERATION

Ingredients

2 green-tea tea bags

⅔ cup loosely packed mint leaves

⅓ cup (75g) caster sugar

2 cups (500ml) boiling water

2 cups ice-cubes

1 medium green apple (150g), unpeeled, sliced thinly crossways

½ cup mint sprigs

1 cup (250ml) gin, chilled (see tip)

1⅓ cups (330ml) granny smith apple juice, chilled

2 tablespoons lime juice

Method

1 Place tea bags in a heatproof jug with mint leaves and sugar. Pour over the boiling water, stir until sugar dissolves; stand for 5 minutes. Strain through a fine sieve into a bowl, pressing down on solids to extract all liquid; discard solids. Refrigerate liquid, covered, until cold.

2 To serve, one-third fill a jug with ice-cubes, top with apple slices and mint sprigs; stir in the tea, gin and apple and lime juices to combine. Pour into small glass tumblers.

TIPPLE TIPS

Gin comes in differing styles, with juniper berry the principle flavour. Choose one with added botanicals (components derived from plants), which will give the cocktail a more rounded, complex taste.

You can prepare this the day before.

GINGER ALE & CITRUS PUNCH

SERVES	PREP TIME
8	15 MINUTES + REFRIGERATION

"Get the party started with a jug of this chilled summer punch. With a kick of Pimm's No. 1, it's perfect for a lazy lunch or an alfresco dinner."

Ingredients

125g strawberries, sliced thinly

1 medium orange (240g), sliced thinly

1 medium lime (90g), sliced thinly

700ml bottle Pimm's No. 1, chilled (see tip)

1 lebanese cucumber (130g), sliced thinly diagonally

1.25 litres (5 cups) chilled dry ginger ale

1 cup loosely packed mint leaves

Method

1 Place strawberries, orange slices, lime slices and Pimm's in a large jug; stir to combine. Cover and refrigerate until needed (overnight, if you like).

2 Just before serving, add cucumber slices to the jug with the ginger ale and mint.

TIPPLE TIP

Pimm's No. 1 is a gin-based drink with both citrus and spice flavours.

WATERMELON STINGER

SERVES

8

PREP + COOK TIME

20 MINUTES
+ REFRIGERATION

Ingredients

You will need to start this recipe the day before.

2 fresh small red chillies, bruised

1¼ cups (310ml) vodka

¾ cup (165g) caster sugar

1 tablespoon finely grated lime zest

2 cups (500ml) water

1kg piece watermelon, cut into thin wedges, chilled

1 cup (250ml) soda water, chilled

½ cup (125ml) lime juice

8 fresh small red chillies, extra

ice-cubes, to serve

¼ cup loosely packed mint leaves

Method

1 Cut bruised chillies in half, lengthways; remove seeds from 1 chilli. Place chillies and vodka in a screw-top jar; refrigerate for 24 hours (or longer if you prefer) to infuse. Discard chillies.

2 Stir sugar, zest and the water in a medium saucepan over low heat until sugar dissolves. Simmer, uncovered, for 10 minutes or until syrup is reduced by half. Cool. Refrigerate until chilled.

3 Blend watermelon, in two batches; strain into a large jug. Stir in sugar syrup, chilli-infused vodka, soda water and lime juice.

4 Cut a slit in the base of each extra chilli; place on the rim of each chilled glass. Half fill glasses with ice-cubes; pour in watermelon mixture. Serve stingers topped with mint leaves.

TIPPLE TIPS

The chilli-infused vodka is also very good with lemonade and crushed coriander roots. Chilli-infused vodka can be made up to 1 month ahead.

Watermelon juice separates on standing, so this recipe is best made close to serving.

For a quick cocktail, replace the sugar syrup and soda water with 2 cups (500ml) lemonade.

OYSTERS WITH
TWO DRESSINGS
(recipe on page 82)

Party
FOOD

I like to offer bite-sized
delicacies when guests arrive.
Hand them around as you
introduce people and keep
the conversation moving
until everyone's seated.

TOMATO TARTS WITH PROSCIUTTO

SERVES

8

PREP + COOK TIME

30 MINUTES

"There's something deliciously decadent about melted cheese, fluffy baked pastry and prosciutto. This upscale pizza is perfect party food."

Ingredients

2 sheets puff pastry

1 egg yolk

½ teaspoon water

1 cup (150g) drained semi-dried tomatoes, chopped finely

1 cup (100g) grated fontina cheese

16 kalamata olives, chopped

5 thin slices prosciutto (75g), cut crossways into thin strips

1 cup (80g) grated parmesan

dried chilli flakes, optional

Method

1 Place a large oven tray (or two smaller trays) in the centre of the oven. Preheat oven to 200°C/180°C fan-forced.

2 Place each pastry sheet on a sheet of baking paper large enough to hold the pastry. Stand at room temperature for 5 minutes or until thawed.

3 With a fork, press a 5mm border around the edge of the pastry. Whisk egg yolk with the water. Brush the egg mixture along the border. Prick the rest of the pastry all over with the fork to keep it from puffing too much. Transfer both pastries, with baking paper, onto the hot baking tray or trays. Bake for 10 minutes or until firm and golden. Remove from the oven and increase the temperature to 230°C/210°C fan-forced.

4 Cool pastry slightly and press gently with a clean tea towel to flatten any large air pockets. Scatter a thin layer of semi-dried tomato over pastry; top with the cheese and olives. Place prosciutto strips on top, then sprinkle with parmesan.

5 Bake for 5 minutes or until the cheese has melted. Cool for a few minutes, then cut into strips or small squares to serve. Add a sprinkle of dried chilli flakes, if you like.

GRILLED PEACH SALAD WITH ORANGE BLOSSOM DRESSING

SERVES

4

PREP + COOK TIME

20 MINUTES

"This gorgeous deconstructed salad will be be a real hit. Just make sure to serve it with cocktail forks and plenty of napkins."

Ingredients

4 large slipstone peaches (880g), halved

4 sprigs rosemary

8 slices prosciutto (120g)

2 tablespoons brown sugar

2 tablespoons caster sugar

80g rocket, trimmed

100g fetta, chopped coarsely

ORANGE BLOSSOM DRESSING

2 tablespoons orange blossom water (see note)

2 tablespoons olive oil

1 tablespoon balsamic vinegar

1 tablespoon pure maple syrup

1 clove garlic, crushed

Method

1 Make orange blossom dressing.
2 Preheat grill. Line two oven trays with foil.
3 Place peach halves and half the rosemary on one tray; place prosciutto and the remaining rosemary on second tray. Sprinkle brown and caster sugars over the peaches and prosciutto. Toss to coat. Spread out into a single layer.
4 Place peaches under hot grill for 8 minutes or until caramelised. Grill prosciutto for 4 minutes or until crisp.

5 Place peaches, prosciutto and rocket on serving plates; top with fetta and drizzle with dressing.

ORANGE BLOSSOM DRESSING

Whisk ingredients in a small bowl until combined. Season to taste.

COOKING NOTES

Orange blossom water, also known as orange flower water, is available from specialty food stores, delicatessens and some health food stores.

The dressing can be made 3 days ahead. Refrigerate until ready to use.

CHICKEN SKEWERS WITH GREEN OLIVE DRESSING

MAKES

24

PREP + COOK TIME

30 MINUTES
+ REFRIGERATION

Ingredients

You will need to soak 24 bamboo skewers in cold water for 30 minutes for this recipe.

4 large chicken thigh fillets (800g)

3 cloves garlic, crushed

2 tablespoons finely chopped oregano

2 teaspoons finely grated lemon zest

2 tablespoons strained lemon juice

2 tablespoons olive oil

lemon wedges, to serve

GREEN OLIVE DRESSING

½ cup (60g) pitted green olives

2 tablespoons oregano leaves

⅓ cup (80ml) olive oil

Method

1 Cut each thigh fillet into 6 long strips; combine with garlic, oregano, zest, juice and oil in a medium bowl. Cover with plastic wrap; refrigerate for 2 hours.
2 Make green olive dressing.
3 Thread one strip of chicken onto each of 24 skewers. Cook chicken skewers, in batches, on a heated oiled grill plate (or barbecue or grill) for 2 minutes each side or until cooked through.
4 Serve chicken skewers with green olive dressing and lemon wedges.

GREEN OLIVE DRESSING
Coarsely chop 4 of the olives; reserve. Blend or process remaining ingredients until almost smooth. Spoon dressing into a serving bowl; top with reserved olives.

COOKING NOTES

Chicken thigh fillets are better to use than chicken breast meat as their higher fat content will ensure that the meat stays moist during barbecuing.

To save time, the chicken can be marinated a day ahead; store, covered, in the fridge.

You will need 2 lemons for this recipe.

MEDITERRANEAN LAMB MEATBALLS WITH WHITE BEAN DIP

MAKES

60

PREP + COOK TIME

40 MINUTES

Ingredients

1kg minced lamb

1½ cups (105g) stale breadcrumbs

1 large red onion (300g), chopped finely

2 tablespoons finely chopped chervil

2 tablespoons finely chopped flat-leaf parsley

2 tablespoons finely chopped mint

2 teaspoons caraway seeds, toasted

1 teaspoon ground cumin

1 teaspoon ground cinnamon

½ teaspoon ground cloves

2 eggs, beaten lightly

¼ cup (60ml) iced water

vegetable oil, for shallow-frying

WHITE BEAN DIP

400g can white beans, rinsed, drained

1 clove garlic, crushed

2 tablespoons extra virgin olive oil

1 tablespoon tahini

2 teaspoons finely grated lemon rind

2 tablespoons lemon juice

1 tablespoon coarsely chopped flat-leaf parsley

Method

1 To make meatballs, place all ingredients, except the oil, in a large bowl, season; mix well to combine. Using damp hands, roll tablespoons of lamb mixture into balls.

2 Fill a large frying pan with 1cm oil; heat over medium heat. Shallow-fry meatballs, in four batches, turning frequently, for 5 minutes or until browned and cooked through. (You will need to replenish the oil slightly with each batch.) Remove meatballs with tongs or a slotted spoon; drain on paper towel.

3 Meanwhile, make white bean dip. Serve meatballs on a platter; accompany with dip.

WHITE BEAN DIP Process ingredients until smooth.

COOKING NOTES

Meatballs can be shaped a day ahead; store, covered, in the fridge.

Meatballs can also be cooked over high heat on a lightly oiled barbecue grill plate, turning frequently, for 7 minutes or until browned and cooked through.

CRISPY CHEESE RAVIOLI

SERVES

6

PREP + COOK TIME

25 MINUTES

"This is the dish that makes you look like a star without really trying. I like to quickly cook these after everyone has arrived, so the cheese is still warm and gooey. Just ask your guests to pass the platter around among themselves. Naughty but nice."

Ingredients

2 eggs, beaten lightly

2 cups (140g) fresh breadcrumbs

vegetable oil, for deep-frying

500g packet good-quality cheese ravioli

1½ cups (400g) good-quality tomato pasta sauce

2 tablespoons chopped basil

chopped flat-leaf parsley or basil, extra

Method

1 Place the egg and breadcrumbs in separate bowls.

2 Half fill a deep-fryer or large saucepan with oil and heat to 190°C (the oil is hot enough when a cube of bread dropped in the oil turns golden in 30 seconds). Dip ravioli in egg, then toss in the breadcrumbs, to coat. Working in batches of five, fry the ravioli for 1–2 minutes or until golden and crisp. Remove with a slotted spoon and drain on paper towel.

3 Meanwhile, heat the pasta sauce in a small saucepan over low heat until hot. Season to taste and stir in basil; transfer to a heatproof serving bowl.

4 Arrange the ravioli on a platter, sprinkle with the extra parsley or basil and serve with the sauce for dipping.

COOKING NOTE

If you prefer not to use a cheese filling, any ravioli works just as well.

POTATO & BACON PIZZA

SERVES

4

PREP + COOK TIME

35 MINUTES

"Slices of pizza make fabulous finger food. And this little potato and bacon beauty is ready in just over half an hour."

Ingredients

2 x 335g pizza bases

2 tablespoons olive oil

4 rindless bacon slices (260g), chopped coarsely

2 cloves garlic, sliced thinly

1 tablespoon coarsely chopped fresh rosemary

½ teaspoon dried chilli flakes

500g potatoes, sliced thinly

1 cup (80g) finely grated parmesan

1 tablespoon rosemary leaves, to garnish

Method

1 Preheat oven to 220°C/200°C fan-forced.

2 Place pizza bases on oven trays; bake for 10 minutes or until crisp.

3 Meanwhile, heat oil in a large frying pan over medium heat; cook bacon, garlic, rosemary and chilli, stirring, for 5 minutes. Remove mixture from pan.

4 Cook potato in same heated pan, stirring frequently, for 10 minutes or until tender.

5 Sprinkle each pizza base with ⅓ cup of the cheese. Divide bacon mixture and potato between bases; top with remaining cheese.

6 Bake pizzas for 5 minutes or until browned lightly; season to taste and serve garnished with rosemary.

COOKING NOTES

I use 25cm diameter, packaged pizza bases for this recipe.

Make sure you slice the potatoes as thinly as possible.

OYSTERS WITH TWO DRESSINGS

MAKES

48

PREP + COOK TIME

10 MINUTES

Ingredients

48 oysters, on the half shell

RED WINE VINEGAR DRESSING
1 tablespoon finely chopped green onions
2 tablespoons red wine vinegar
2 teaspoons extra virgin olive oil

SPICY LIME DRESSING
2 tablespoons lime juice
2 tablespoons japanese soy sauce
1 teaspoon white sugar
1 fresh small red chilli, chopped finely

Method

1 Make red wine vinegar dressing.
2 Make spicy lime dressing.
3 Just before serving, drizzle half the oysters with red wine vinegar dressing and the remaining oysters with spicy lime dressing.

RED WINE VINEGAR DRESSING
Place ingredients in a screw-top jar, season to taste; shake well.

SPICY LIME DRESSING Place ingredients in a screw-top jar, season to taste; shake well.

COOKING NOTES

Oysters are ideally served on a bed of crushed ice (especially in the summer), or nestled on a platter with a bed of rock salt to prevent them from sliding around.

If you don't want to serve oysters on the half shell, you can place single oysters on Chinese soup spoons, then top them with the different dressings.

GREEK BARBECUED LAMB WITH SPICY YOGHURT DRESSING

MAKES

16

PREP + COOK TIME

40 MINUTES
+ REFRIGERATION

Ingredients

You will need to soak 16 bamboo skewers in cold water for 30 minutes for this recipe.

1.5kg boneless lamb leg, fat-trimmed, cut into 2cm cubes

¼ cup coarsely chopped oregano

2 tablespoons dried oregano

4 cloves garlic, chopped finely

½ cup (125ml) olive oil

1 tablespoon balsamic glaze

1 medium lemon (140g), cut into cheeks

1 tablespoon flat-leaf parsley, to garnish

SPICY YOGHURT DRESSING

1 cup (280g) greek-style yoghurt

1 teaspoon ground cumin

2 cloves garlic, crushed

¼ cup (60ml) water

1 fresh long red chilli, seeds removed, chopped finely

Method

1 Combine lamb, fresh and dried oregano, garlic and olive oil in a medium bowl. Cover; refrigerate for 3 hours or overnight.
2 Preheat a barbecue to medium-high. Thread lamb onto skewers; season. Cook skewers on barbecue, turning, for 5 minutes or until cooked as desired.
3 Meanwhile, make the spicy yoghurt dressing.

4 Place skewers on a serving platter; drizzle with balsamic glaze. Serve with yoghurt dressing and lemon cheeks. Sprinkle with parsley, to serve.

SPICY YOGHURT DRESSING
Combine yoghurt, cumin, garlic, the water and half the chilli. To serve, sprinkle with black pepper and remaining chilli.

GREEK BARBECUED LAMB WITH
SPICY YOGHURT DRESSING
(recipe previous page)

GARLIC & CHILLI MUSSELS

SERVES

4

PREP + COOK TIME

20 MINUTES

> "This colourful dish is perfect to share. Just give everyone a little fork and let them help themselves. The mussels are perfectly complemented by the heat of the chilli and the buttery garlic."

Ingredients

60g butter, chopped

3 cloves garlic, chopped finely

1 fresh long red chilli, sliced thinly

⅓ cup (80ml) dry white wine

1kg small black mussels, scrubbed, bearded

⅓ cup coarsely chopped flat-leaf parsley

Method

1 Heat butter, garlic and chilli in a large saucepan over medium heat, stirring, until fragrant.
2 Add wine to pan; bring to the boil. Add mussels; cover with a tight-fitting lid. Cook for 5 minutes, shaking pan occasionally, or until mussels open. Stir in parsley; season to taste.

serving suggestion Serve with crusty bread or a bowl of French fries.

COOKING NOTES

To save time, you can buy pre-cleaned, bearded mussels.

It's a cooking myth that unopened mussels should be discarded. If you can pry them open, they are safe to eat. The reason they don't open is simply due to how the shell has formed.

SPINACH & GINGER DUMPLINGS WITH SPICY DRESSING

SERVES

4

PREP + COOK TIME

30 MINUTES

Ingredients

240g english spinach

227g canned water chestnuts, drained, chopped finely

2 green onions, chopped finely

4cm piece fresh ginger (20g), grated finely

1 tablespoon light soy sauce

1 egg, beaten lightly

24 gow gee wrappers (230g)

450g firm tofu, sliced thickly

2 tablespoons vegetable oil

2 teaspoons sesame seeds, toasted

½ cup loosely packed coriander leaves

SPICY DRESSING

½ cup (125ml) chinese black vinegar (see note)

1 tablespoon lemon juice

1 teaspoon sesame oil

1 fresh small red chilli, sliced thinly

Method

1 Make spicy dressing.

2 Place spinach in a medium heatproof bowl, cover with boiling water; drain immediately. Refresh under cold running water; drain. When cool enough to handle, squeeze excess water from spinach; chop finely.

3 Combine spinach, water chestnuts, onion, ginger, soy sauce and egg in a bowl. Place 2 teaspoons of the mixture in the centre of a wrapper, leaving a 1cm border; brush the edge with water. Fold wrapper over filling; pleat the edge to seal. Repeat with the remaining spinach mixture and wrappers.

4 Cook dumplings in a large saucepan of boiling water, in three batches, for 3 minutes or until cooked through. Drain; keep warm.

5 Meanwhile, pat tofu dry with paper towel. Heat oil in a large frying pan over high heat; cook tofu for 2 minutes each side or until golden.

6 Place tofu and dumplings on a serving platter; drizzle with dressing, then sprinkle with sesame seeds and coriander.

SPICY DRESSING Combine ingredients in a small bowl.

COOKING NOTES

Chinese black vinegar is made from fermented glutinous rice, is mildly acidic and slightly sweet, and is used as a condiment. You can buy it at Asian food stores (the Chinkiang brand is one of the best). You can use rice vinegar instead.

Pleating the edge of the dumplings can be a little tricky. You can simply press the edges together to ensure they are well sealed – they will be just as tasty.

LEEK & FETTA FILLO CIGARS

MAKES

20

PREP + COOK TIME

50 MINUTES

"A great party starter, this can be made in advance, set aside and just popped into the oven when people start arriving. The salty, flavoursome fetta mixed with buttery leek is a brilliant combination, especially when wrapped in light, crispy fillo pastry."

Ingredients

80g butter

1 medium leek (350g), halved, sliced thinly

220g greek fetta, crumbled

1 small handful chopped flat-leaf parsley

10 sheets fillo pastry, halved crossways

Method

1 Melt 20g of the butter in a medium frying pan over medium heat. Add leek; cook, stirring, for 5 minutes or until soft. Transfer to a bowl; cool.

2 Add the fetta and parsley to the leek; mix until well combined.

3 Preheat the oven to 180°C/160°C fan-forced. Line an oven tray with baking paper.

4 Microwave remaining butter in a small microwave-safe bowl on high power for 30 seconds or until melted. Brush 1 sheet of pastry lightly with the melted butter. Fold in half lengthways. Place 1 tablespoon of the leek mixture at the short end, leaving a 2cm border. Fold in the sides and roll up firmly to enclose.

5 Place, seam-side down, on prepared tray. Brush with a little butter. Repeat with the remaining fillo, butter and leek mixture.

6 Bake fillo cigars for 15 minutes or until golden. Serve immediately.

SETTING THE Scene

You can completely transform
a room with the right lighting,
decorations, tableware and music.
When entertaining friends,
I like to think creatively...

DINING TABLE

Express your style and create the "wow factor" by making your tabletop work with the mood of the occasion. Your dining table should be inviting and present a clear reflection of your style. It's ideal if your table sits six to 10 people and has chairs that are comfortable but not too laid-back. Mix coverings, styles, colours and materials in your dining room until you strike the right balance of festivity and functionality.

Seating

I LIKE TO ENTERTAIN WITH EVEN NUMBERS AND A TABLE SMALL ENOUGH TO BE ABLE TO CARRY ONE CONVERSATION. I BELIEVE THE HOST SHOULD SIT AT THE CENTRE OF THE TABLE TO HELP THE CONVERSATION FLOW AND KEEP AN EYE ON WHO'S BEING LEFT OUT.

Table coverings

A CRISP, FRESHLY IRONED LINEN TABLECLOTH AND NAPKINS CAN BE USED FOR FORMAL OCCASIONS, WHILE RUNNERS SHOW OFF CENTREPIECES, AND PLACEMATS ADD INTERESTING TEXTURES.

DINNERWARE

You need a set of matching plates for main meals; smaller plates for entrées, bread and sides; large serving platters; and matching cutlery, including steak knives and dessert spoons and forks. I like wooden pepper grinders and sea salt in mini dishes. When serving warm dishes, I preheat plates in the microwave on HIGH for a minute or warm them in the oven.

CANDLES

Look for impressive candle holders, lanterns, glass vases and candelabra that will help create a beautiful subtle light. Keep in mind the height of your candles so they don't interfere with conversation across the table. Freeze candles the day before so they last longer and to stop the wax from overflowing.

Lighting

FOR EVENING OCCASIONS, IT'S IMPORTANT TO GET THE LIGHT RIGHT. TAKE IT FROM ME, PEOPLE LOOK AND FEEL BETTER IN FLATTERING LIGHT, SO BUY SOME LAMPS AND LOWER THE WATTAGE.

MUSIC

Music is central to creating ambience and underpins the entire mood. Have playlists sorted in advance. I like to set up music to continue from when guests arrive to when they leave.

DECORATIONS

FLOWERS
Brighten your table with fresh flowers, cut low so guests can easily see over them. Choose less fragrant flowers so they don't interfere with the aroma of the food.

CENTREPIECES
Because centrepieces should remain on the table for the duration of the meal, keep them minimal if you plan on serving large platters. Also keep them low so they don't get in the way of good conversation.

HERB POTS
Most greengrocers and nurseries have mini herb pots for sale. Dress them up with brown paper and arrange them down the centre of your table. You can pop place cards in them and then your guests can take them home as a living memory of the special occasion that you hosted.

CUSHIONS
When shopping, keep an eye out for cushions to brighten up existing chairs. Coordinate with colour and think about what shades and tones you want to highlight in your dining room.

PRELOVED PIECES
Take a wander around your local market and you'll be amazed at what you can find: old lanterns, offbeat candle holders, candlesticks and baskets.

NATURAL LOOK
Go back to nature and add colour and form with creative settings featuring wooden bowls and platters loaded with grapes, apples, chillies, dried fruit and pine cones.

STONES & SHELLS
I love a collection of seashells that brings that relaxed beach feeling into the dining room. Polished black or natural stones look good on napkins, or you can write on them for place names.

GIFTS
Candles, scented body scrubs, bath bombs, jars of olives, jams, chocolates and beautiful soaps are simple, inexpensive gifts for Christmas or other occasions. You can even make them yourself.

BATHROOM
Dress up with fresh flowers, scented candles, fluffy hand towels and soap pumps.

Italian

Why not host an Italian-themed dinner and ask guests to bring along their favourite Italian wine and cheese to talk about over dinner? This is an inexpensive and easy all-year-round theme and anyone can do it. Traditional Italian dishes are easy to prepare and your guests can rate the wines and cheeses over dinner.

SETTING

Ideas include a red-and-white chequered tablecloth, floral arrangement in a wooden box and mini terracotta pots with fresh herbs. In summer, dine alfresco with candle lanterns lighting up the garden.

MUSIC

MY PLAYLIST HAS A MIX OF ITALIAN OPERA AND VENICE BAROQUE FOR ARRIVALS TO ENTRÉES, AND DEAN MARTIN AND 1960S VIVA ITALIA DANCE MUSIC FOR DANCING AFTER DESSERT.

FOOD

If you haven't tried my crispy ravioli, this is your night. Follow it up with creamy, mouth-watering gnocchi and finish with a slightly fruity pana cotta. It doesn't get more Italian than that!

Italian
MENU

Crispy Cheese Ravioli (page 78)

Creamy Mushroom & Spinach Gnocchi (page 112)

Clove Panna Cotta with Fresh Figs (page 183)

Mediterranean

This summer theme is centred on foods and festivities of the Greek Islands. Start with chilled Mojitos, grilled haloumi and bowls of tzatziki. Highlights might include a shot of Ouzo after lunch, Greek holiday music and dancing into the evening. This is a great theme for hot weather. Wear cool white linens to show off your tan.

Here's your chance to dress up and pay a visit to a past era. Choose from the Roaring Twenties, the glamorous '50s, flower-powered '60s, psychedelic '70s and the big, bold and brassy '80s.

1960s

Inspiration: *The Party* with Peter Sellers, *Mad Men*, James Bond, flower power.

Music: The Beatles, the Rolling Stones, Woodstock festival.

Dress Code: Bell-bottom jeans, paisley shirts, high boots, miniskirts.

Serve: Dry martinis, Beef Wellington, creamed spinach.

1970s

Inspiration: *Saturday Night Fever*, *Starsky & Hutch*, *Dirty Harry*, *Hawaii Five-O*.

Music: Disco, the Bee Gees, Donna Summer, ABBA.

Dress Code: Big collars, safari suits, tight shirts, hippie gear.

Serve: Champagne punch, prawn cocktails, cheese and beef fondues, key lime pie.

1980s

Inspiration: TV shows *Miami Vice, Dynasty, Dallas*.

Music: Madonna, Duran Duran, Human League, Blondie, Kiss, Queen, AC/DC.

Dress Code: Gold and copper tones, sequins, big shoulder pads, parachute pants.

Serve: Cosmopolitans, chicken scaloppini, sticky date pudding.

SANG CHOI BAU
(recipe page 124)

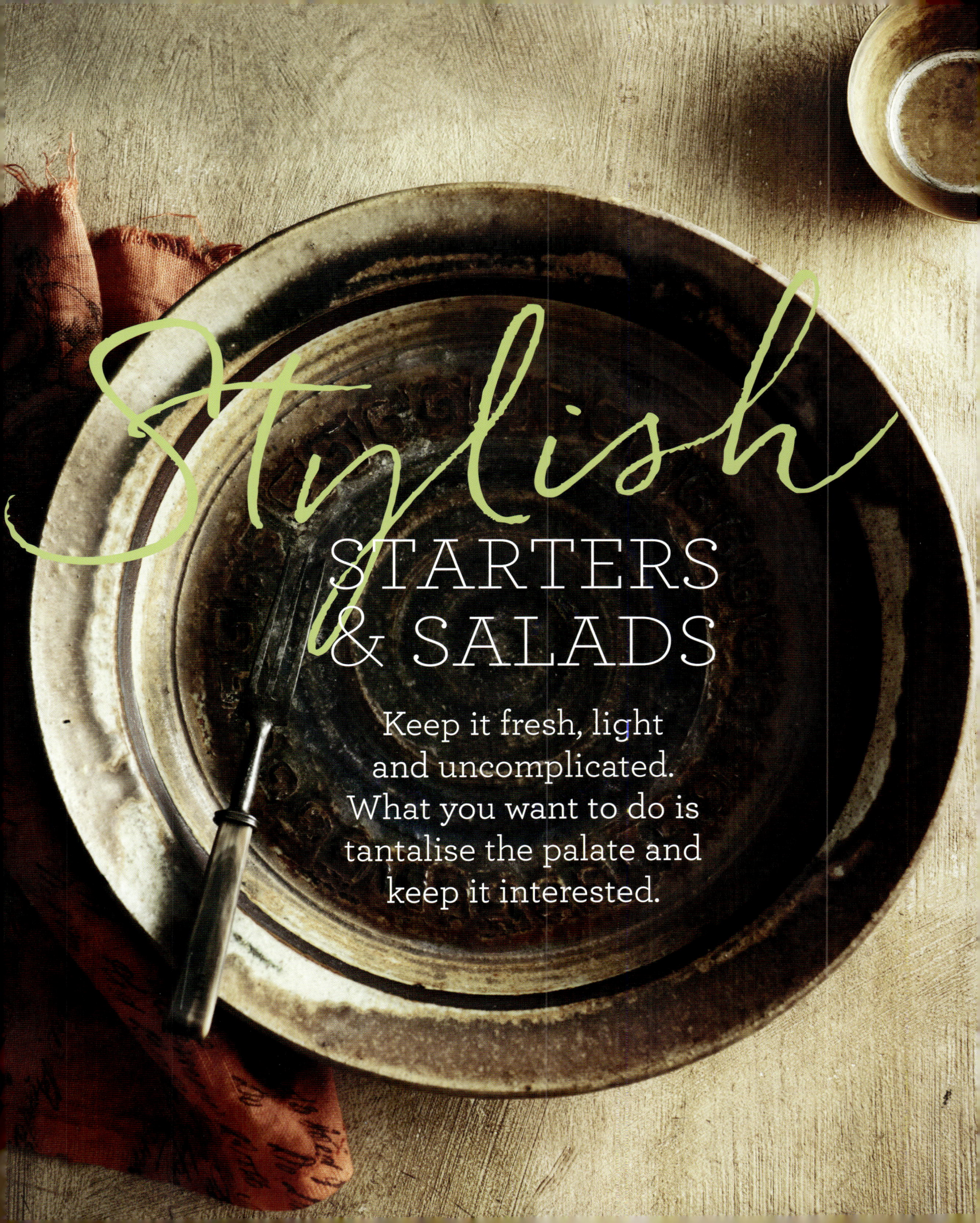

Stylish

STARTERS & SALADS

Keep it fresh, light
and uncomplicated.
What you want to do is
tantalise the palate and
keep it interested.

PRAWN & ASPARAGUS RISOTTO

Ingredients

500g uncooked medium king prawns

3 cups (750ml) chicken stock

3 cups (750ml) water

15g butter

1 tablespoon olive oil

1 small brown onion (80g), chopped finely

2 cups (400g) arborio rice

½ cup (125ml) dry sherry

15g butter, extra

2 teaspoons olive oil, extra

2 cloves garlic, crushed

500g asparagus, chopped coarsely

⅓ cup (25g) coarsely grated parmesan

⅓ cup loosely packed basil leaves

Method

1 Shell and devein prawns, leaving tails intact.

2 Place stock and the water in a large saucepan; bring to the boil. Reduce heat to low; simmer, covered.

3 Meanwhile, heat butter and oil in a large saucepan over medium heat; cook onion, stirring, for 2 minutes or until softened. Add rice; stir to coat the rice in onion mixture. Add sherry; cook, stirring, until liquid is almost absorbed.

4 Stir in 1 cup of simmering stock mixture; cook, stirring, over low heat until liquid is absorbed. Continue adding stock mixture, in 1-cup batches, stirring, until absorbed after each addition. Total cooking time should be about 35 minutes or until the rice is tender.

5 Heat extra butter and extra oil in a medium frying pan; cook prawns and garlic, stirring, until prawns just change colour.

6 Meanwhile, boil, steam or microwave asparagus until just tender; drain.

7 Add asparagus, prawn mixture and cheese to risotto; cook, stirring, until cheese melts. Season to taste. Serve risotto sprinkled with basil.

SMOKED SALMON RÖSTI STACKS WITH BUTTERMILK DRESSING

SERVES

4

PREP + COOK TIME

40 MINUTES + COOLING

"A delicious entrée, this looks impressive plated up and served at any table. I love it when colour and flavour combine well together to bring out the best of each ingredient. This packs some seriously good flavours."

Ingredients

800g medium potatoes, unpeeled, washed

2 tablespoons olive oil

100g smoked salmon slices

40g baby rocket leaves

BUTTERMILK DRESSING

⅓ cup (80ml) buttermilk

1 tablespoon prepared horseradish

1 tablespoon finely chopped fresh flat-leaf parsley

Method

1 Boil or steam whole potatoes for 5 minutes; drain. Cool for 20 minutes.

2 Meanwhile, make buttermilk dressing.

3 Coarsely grate potatoes into a medium bowl. Season.

4 Heat oil in a large frying pan over medium heat; drop ¼ cups of grated potato into pan, flatten with a spatula. Cook the rösti, in batches, for 4 minutes each side or until browned and crisp. Remove from pan. Drain on paper towel.

5 Layer rösti, salmon and rocket on serving plates; serve with buttermilk dressing.

BUTTERMILK DRESSING
Combine ingredients in a small bowl.

CREAMY MUSHROOM & SPINACH GNOCCHI

SERVES

4

PREP + COOK TIME

10 MINUTES

"I fell in love with gnocchi when I lived in Milan many moons ago, while I was working there as a model. I would meet my friends at a trattoria run by a big Italian family and 'Mamma' would lovingly make melt-in-your-mouth gnocchi. The dish here has it all – tender gnocchi, wonderful wilted spinach and the creamiest mushroom sauce."

Ingredients

625g fresh potato gnocchi

375g assorted mushrooms, sliced thinly

2 cloves garlic, crushed

300ml pouring cream

90g baby spinach leaves

⅓ cup (25g) freshly grated parmesan

Method

1 Cook the gnocchi in a large saucepan of boiling water until tender; drain.

2 Meanwhile, cook mushroom and garlic in a heated, oiled large frying pan over medium heat, stirring, for 2 minutes or until softened. Add the cream and spinach; bring to the boil. Reduce heat; simmer, uncovered, for 3 minutes or until the sauce thickens slightly. Stir in half the parmesan. Season to taste.

3 Add gnocchi to pan; stir gently. Serve gnocchi topped with remaining parmesan.

COOKING NOTE

Try using a variety of mushrooms, such as flat, button and portobello.

PRAWN & AVOCADO STACKS WITH BASIL OIL

SERVES

4

PREP + COOK TIME

50 MINUTES

Ingredients

1 medium red capsicum (200g)

2 medium avocados (500g), chopped finely

1 medium tomato (150g), seeded, chopped finely

2 tablespoons lime juice

1 tablespoon finely chopped coriander

¼ cup (60ml) extra virgin olive oil

¼ small red onion (25g), chopped finely

1 fresh small red chilli, seeds removed, chopped finely

12 uncooked medium king prawns (540g), shelled and deveined, tails intact

1 clove garlic, chopped finely

¼ cup small basil leaves

BASIL OIL

1 cup loosely packed basil leaves

½ cup (125ml) olive oil

Method

1 Heat barbecue grill (or grill pan or grill) to hot. Cook capsicum, turning occasionally, for 15 minutes or until skin blisters and blackens. Remove from heat, cover with plastic; stand for 5 minutes. Peel away skins; discard seeds and membranes. Chop capsicum finely.

2 Make basil oil.

3 Combine capsicum, avocado, tomato, half the juice, coriander, 1 tablespoon of the oil, onion and chilli in a bowl; season to taste.

4 Place a ring mould on each of four serving plates. Divide avocado mixture between moulds and press gently with the back of a spoon to level. Remove moulds.

5 Heat a barbecue hotplate to medium-high. Combine prawns with garlic and 1 tablespoon of the remaining oil in a medium bowl; cook until changed in colour. Drizzle with remaining juice and remaining oil. Place prawns on top of avocado stacks. Drizzle with basil oil; top with basil leaves.

BASIL OIL Blanch the basil in a small saucepan of boiling water for 1 second; drain. Refresh basil in a bowl of iced water; drain well. Place basil on paper towel or clean Chux and squeeze out as much liquid as possible. Blend basil with oil, adding oil in a thin, steady stream until smooth. Season to taste.

COOKING NOTE

To make these impressive-looking stacks, use four 6-8cm ring moulds or an empty, cleaned 7cm tin can with both ends removed.

SCALLOP & ROCKET SALAD WITH BALSAMIC DRESSING

SERVES

4

PREP + COOK TIME

15 MINUTES

Ingredients

12 scallops without roe (300g)

75g baby rocket leaves

1 lebanese cucumber (130g), sliced thinly lengthways

1 tablespoon sesame seeds, toasted

1 lime, cut into wedges

BALSAMIC DRESSING

1 tablespoon balsamic vinegar

1 teaspoon olive oil

1 teaspoon lime juice

pinch of white sugar

Method

1 Make balsamic dressing.

2 Pat scallops dry with paper towel. Cook scallops on a heated oiled grill pan (or barbecue or grill) over high heat until browned lightly on both sides. Remove from heat; cover to keep warm.

3 Place rocket, cucumber and dressing in a medium bowl; toss gently to combine.

4 Divide salad among serving plates; top with the scallops and sesame seeds. Serve with lime wedges.

BALSAMIC DRESSING Place ingredients in a screw-top jar, season to taste; shake well.

COOKING NOTES

Always choose fresh scallops rather than frozen ones, as the frozen scallops are gorged with water and tend to stew rather than grill when cooked.

Use a vegetable peeler to slice the cucumber thinly into ribbons.

SALMON CARPACCIO

SERVES

8

PREP + COOK TIME

20 MINUTES
+ REFRIGERATION

"This is such an elegant dish to share and it looks beautiful served on a large white platter. The trick is to choose a perfect fillet of salmon, one that's bright in colour, with not too many white lines in the flesh."

Ingredients

½ **medium green capsicum (100g), chopped finely**

2 **green onions (scallions), chopped finely**

400g **piece sashimi salmon, sliced thinly (see note)**

1 **tablespoon fresh dill sprigs**

2 **tablespoons lime juice**

2 **tablespoons extra virgin olive oil**

Method

1 Combine capsicum and onion in a small bowl.
2 Arrange salmon slices on a large serving plate. Sprinkle capsicum mixture and dill over salmon. Drizzle salmon with juice, then oil. Season.
3 Cover salmon; refrigerate for 1 hour.

serving suggestion Scatter mixed micro leaves and edible flowers over salmon and serve with thinly sliced toasted bread.

COOKING NOTE

Freezing the piece of salmon for about 1 hour will make it easier to slice. You can then finely slice the partly frozen fish using a mandoline or a V-slicer.

CREAM OF ZUCCHINI SOUP

SERVES

4

PREP + COOK TIME

35 MINUTES
+ COOLING

"This delightful soup, finished off with a swirl of cream and sprinkling of chives, is so simple to whip up."

Ingredients

30g butter

1 large brown onion (200g), chopped finely

2 cloves garlic, crushed

2 tablespoons plain flour

8 large zucchini (1.2kg), chopped coarsely

1½ cups (375ml) vegetable stock

1 cup (250ml) water

½ cup (125ml) pouring cream

1 tablespoon pouring cream, extra

1 tablespoon coarsely chopped chives

Method

1 Melt butter in a large saucepan over medium heat; cook onion and garlic, stirring, until onion softens. Add flour and zucchini; cook, stirring, for 2 minutes.

2 Stir in stock and the water; bring to the boil. Reduce heat; simmer, uncovered, for 15 minutes or until zucchini is tender. Cool for 10 minutes.

3 Blend or process soup, in batches, until smooth.

4 Just before serving, return soup to pan. Add cream; stir over medium heat until hot. Season to taste. To serve, drizzle with extra cream and sprinkle with chives.

COOKING NOTES

Recipe is not suitable to freeze.

Don't reboil the soup once you add the cream, as the soup may curdle.

QUINOA SALAD WITH HALOUMI & POMEGRANATE

SERVES

4

PREP + COOK TIME

25 MINUTES

"This salad with nutty quinoa has the flavours of warming spices, sour and sweet pomegranate, salty cheese and tangy yoghurt all dancing together."

Ingredients

1 cup (200g) red or white quinoa

2 cups (500ml) water

1 clove garlic, crushed

2 tablespoons lemon juice

2 teaspoons ground cumin

2 teaspoons ground coriander

¼ cup (60ml) olive oil

½ cup loosely packed mint leaves

100g baby spinach leaves

½ cup (75g) sunflower seeds, toasted

250g haloumi, cut into 1cm slices

¾ cup (210g) greek-style yoghurt

⅓ cup (50g) pomegranate seeds

Method

1 Bring quinoa and the water to the boil in a medium saucepan; cook, covered, over low heat for 15 minutes or until tender. Drain; cool slightly.

2 Combine the garlic, juice, spices and 1 tablespoon of the oil in a large bowl; season to taste. Add the quinoa to bowl with mint, spinach and seeds; toss gently to combine.

3 Heat the remaining oil in a large frying pan over high heat; cook haloumi for 1 minute each side or until golden.

4 Serve the quinoa salad topped with haloumi, yoghurt and pomegranate seeds.

COOKING NOTES

Cut a whole pomegranate in half and scrape the seeds from flesh with your fingers while holding the pomegranate upside down in a bowl of cold water. The seeds will sink and the white pith will float.

Make sure you cook the haloumi just before serving, as it becomes tough and rubbery on cooling.

SANG CHOI BAU

SERVES	PREP + COOK TIME
4	30 MINUTES

"This classic dish ticks all the boxes – fresh Asian flavours, a good hit of protein and some serious crunch factor. In fact, I don't know anyone who doesn't love Sang Choi Bau. You can swap the chicken for beef or pork mince, if you like. They work just as well."

Ingredients

1 tablespoon peanut oil

2 teaspoons grated fresh ginger

2 cloves garlic, crushed

300g chicken mince

6 green onions, chopped finely

2 tablespoons oyster sauce

2 tablespoons soy sauce

2 tablespoons fresh lime juice

½ cup chopped coriander leaves

1 cup (80g) bean sprouts, trimmed

8–12 medium iceberg lettuce leaves, to serve

oyster sauce, extra

Method

1 Heat the oil in a wok over medium-high heat. Add ginger and garlic; stir-fry for 1 minute or until fragrant.

2 Add mince; stir-fry until mince is cooked through. Add onion, sauces and juice; stir-fry for a further 2 minutes or until combined. Remove from the heat; stir in coriander leaves and bean sprouts.

3 Spoon the mixture into individual lettuce leaves. Drizzle with a little more oyster sauce, then serve immediately.

CRUNCHY SALT & PEPPER PRAWNS WITH SWEET CHILLI SYRUP

SERVES

6

PREP + COOK TIME

45 MINUTES
+ STANDING

Ingredients

30 uncooked medium prawns (800g)

¾ cup (55g) panko (japanese) breadcrumbs

1 teaspoon cracked black pepper

1½ teaspoons peri peri seasoning

2 teaspoons sea salt flakes

2 egg whites, beaten lightly

vegetable oil, for deep-frying

1 fresh long red chilli, sliced thinly

2 tablespoons coriander leaves

1 green onion, sliced diagonally

SWEET CHILLI SYRUP

½ cup (110g) white sugar

½ cup (125ml) water

¼ cup (80g) sweet chilli sauce

4 kaffir lime leaves, torn

1cm piece fresh ginger (5g), sliced thinly

2 coriander roots and stems, washed, sliced thinly

Method

1 Make sweet chilli syrup.

2 Shell and devein prawns, leaving tails intact.

3 Combine breadcrumbs, pepper, seasoning and salt in a small bowl. Holding prawns by the tail, dip one at a time into egg white, then coat in crumb mixture.

4 Fill a large saucepan or deep-fryer one-third full with oil; heat to 180°C (or until a cube of bread turns golden in 10 seconds). Deep-fry prawns, in batches, for 1 minute or until cooked through and crisp. Remove with a slotted spoon; drain on a paper towel.

5 Arrange prawns on platters, then top with chilli, coriander and green onion. Serve with sweet chilli syrup for dipping.

SWEET CHILLI SYRUP Stir ingredients in a small saucepan over medium heat until sugar dissolves. Bring to the boil. Reduce heat; simmer, uncovered, for 5 minutes or until sauce thickens slightly. Remove from heat; stand for 15 minutes. Discard lime leaves.

COOKING NOTE

The sauce can be made up to 2 days ahead; store, covered, in the fridge. Prawns can be crumbed 3 hours ahead; store, covered, in the fridge.

SCALLOP & MINT RISOTTO

SERVES

6

PREP + COOK TIME

45 MINUTES

"Seared scallops, mint and parmesan are a fabulous combo. Pan-fried in olive oil and butter, the scallops are a bit of an indulgence, but you only live once! Serve with a crisp green salad and a chilled, dry riesling."

Ingredients

3 cups (750ml) chicken or vegetable stock

¼ cup (60ml) olive oil

6 green onions, sliced thinly

1 cup (200g) arborio rice

½ cup (125ml) white wine

50g unsalted butter

18 large scallops, split into 36 rounds, or 36 small scallops

½ cup (40g) finely grated parmesan, romano or pecorino

2 tablespoons chopped mint leaves

micro herbs, to serve

Method

1 Bring the stock to the boil in a medium saucepan over high heat. Reduce heat to low; cover to keep warm.

2 Heat 2 tablespoons of the oil in a medium saucepan over medium heat. Add onion; cook, stirring, for 1 minute. Add rice and stir for 1 minute to coat the grains. Add wine; cook until almost absorbed. Add the hot stock, a ladleful at a time, stirring constantly, allowing each to be absorbed before adding the next. Cooking time should be about 20 minutes or until all the liquid is absorbed and the rice is cooked but still firm to the bite.

3 When the rice is almost cooked (about 4 minutes to go), heat a non-stick, heavy-based large frying pan over high heat until smoking. Reduce the heat to medium-high; add the remaining oil and the butter to pan. Swirl pan to melt. Cook the scallops, in small batches, for 1 minute each side or until golden and just opaque. Cover to keep warm.

4 When the rice is tender, stir in the parmesan and mint; season to taste.

5 Divide risotto among warmed plates and pile the scallops on top. Serve immediately, scattered with micro herbs.

PRIMAVERA SOUP WITH PANGRATTATO

SERVES

4

PREP + COOK TIME

25 MINUTES

"With its lovely combination of greens and delicate pasta, this soup is a favourite. The crunchy pangrattato finishes it off beautifully."

Ingredients

30g butter

4 green onions (100g), chopped

1 litre (4 cups) vegetable stock

2 cups (500ml) water

⅓ cup (75g) risoni pasta

250g baby green zucchini, halved lengthways

150g asparagus, cut into 3cm lengths

2 cups (240g) fresh or frozen baby peas

PANGRATTATO

200g crusty italian bread

2 tablespoons extra virgin olive oil

1 fresh long red chilli, sliced thinly

2 cloves garlic, chopped

⅓ cup loosely packed small flat-leaf parsley leaves

1 teaspoon finely grated lemon zest

Method

1 Heat butter in a large saucepan over medium heat; cook onion, stirring, for 3 minutes or until soft.

2 Add stock and the water to pan; bring to the boil. Add pasta and zucchini; simmer, uncovered, for 5 minutes, stirring occasionally.

3 Meanwhile, make pangrattato.

4 Add asparagus and peas to soup; simmer, uncovered, for 5 minutes or until just tender. Season to taste.

5 Ladle soup into serving bowls; top with pangrattato.

PANGRATTATO Remove crust from bread; tear into 1cm pieces. Heat oil in a large frying pan over medium-high heat; cook chilli and bread pieces, stirring, until browned lightly and crisp. Add garlic; cook until fragrant. Remove from heat; stir in parsley and zest. Season to taste.

COOKING NOTES

This soup is best made just before serving as it will discolour on standing.

If you can't find baby zucchini, use medium-sized zucchini sliced very thinly.

FIG, ROCKET, BLUE CHEESE & CRISPY PROSCIUTTO SALAD

SERVES

4

PREP + COOK TIME

15 MINUTES

Ingredients

1 tablespoon olive oil

12 slices prosciutto (180g)

120g baby rocket leaves

6 ripe figs (360g), quartered

100g blue cheese, crumbled

DRESSING

1 tablespoon red wine vinegar

½ teaspoon dijon mustard

¼ cup (60ml) extra virgin olive oil

Method

1 Heat oil in a large frying pan over medium heat; cook prosciutto for 2 minutes each side or until crisp. Drain on paper towel. Break prosciutto into pieces.

2 Make dressing.

3 Combine rocket, fig, cheese and prosciutto in a shallow serving bowl; drizzle with dressing. Gently toss salad to combine. Season with salt and pepper. Serve immediately.

DRESSING Combine ingredients in a screw-top jar; shake well.

COOKING NOTES

The dressing can be made 1 day ahead; store in the fridge.

If figs are out of season, then you can use thinly sliced rockmelon or grilled mushrooms.

"I want you to embrace entertaining at home. With a bit of creativity, you can be the host with the most, so have a go and give it your best shot."

GREEN SALAD WITH RUSTIC CROUTONS

SERVES

4

PREP + COOK TIME

15 MINUTES

Ingredients

5 slices multigrain bread (180g)

150g green beans, trimmed

170g asparagus, halved lengthways, if large

⅔ cup (80g) fresh or frozen peas

1 medium ripe avocado (250g)

2 tablespoons lemon juice

½ cup (130g) basil pesto

1 tablespoon water

3 cups (90g) loosely packed, trimmed watercress sprigs

Method

1 Preheat a grill plate (or grill or barbecue) over medium-high heat. Remove crusts from bread and tear into bite-sized pieces. Toast bread on the grill plate for 1 minute or until golden.

2 Add the beans to a medium saucepan of boiling salted water; boil, uncovered, for 1 minute. Add asparagus to the same pan; boil for 1½ minutes. Add peas; boil for a further 1 minute or until bright green. Drain; place in a large bowl of iced water to cool. Drain well.

3 Cut avocado in half, remove seed. Squeeze flesh out of each half; drizzle with 1 tablespoon of juice.

4 Place pesto in a large bowl; stir in the water and remaining juice. Add bread, beans, asparagus and peas, then watercress; toss gently to coat. Season to taste.

5 Transfer salad to a serving platter; top with avocado and a sprinkling of black pepper.

COOKING NOTES

Any flavoured pesto, such as rocket, can be used in place of basil pesto.

You will need a bunch of watercress that weighs about 350g.

ASPARAGUS RAVIOLI WITH TOASTED ALMONDS

SERVES

8

PREP + COOK TIME

30 MINUTES

"With a serious 'wow' factor, this dish will really impress your guests! Sprinkling with toasted almonds before serving pulls the flavours together beautifully. If you're in the mood to make more, the ravioli freezes well."

Ingredients

500g thick asparagus

¾ cup ricotta

¾ cup (60g) freshly grated parmesan

2 tablespoons finely chopped basil leaves

2 cloves garlic, chopped finely

pinch of chilli flakes

80 wonton wrappers

200g unsalted butter

½ cup (80g) blanched almonds, chopped

grated or flaked parmesan, extra

finely grated lemon zest

Method

1 Remove and reserve the tips from the asparagus. Bring a small saucepan of salted water to the boil. Cook the asparagus tips for 1 minute or until tender. Drain in a colander and run under cold water until cooled; drain well.

2 Trim the remaining asparagus stalks; process until finely chopped.

3 Add the ricotta, parmesan, basil, garlic and chilli to the chopped asparagus; mix well. Season to taste.

4 Arrange 20 wonton wrappers on a work surface. Place 1 level teaspoon of the asparagus filling in the centre of each wrapper. Using a pastry brush, moisten the edges with water. Top each with another wrapper and press the edges firmly to seal, expelling any air bubbles as you go. Place on a tray lined with baking paper and cover with a damp tea towel. Repeat with remaining wonton wrappers and filling.

(If you don't plan to cook the ravioli immediately, cover with a damp cloth and store in the fridge for up to 2 days.)

5 Bring a large saucepan of well-salted water to the boil. Meanwhile, melt the butter in a frying pan over medium heat and cook until butter turns light brown. Add the almonds, shaking the pan, then immediately transfer to a small heatproof bowl. Cover to keep warm.

6 Add the ravioli to the boiling water in small batches. When they rise to the surface, after about 1 minute, use a slotted spoon to transfer them to warm plates or pasta bowls. (Don't overcook the ravioli or they will start to fall apart.)

7 Spoon the butter mixture over the ravioli. Top with the reserved asparagus tips, a grinding of pepper and a sprinkling of extra parmesan and zest.

GREEN APPLE SLAW

SERVES

6

PREP + COOK TIME

15 MINUTES

"This lovely fresh salad is so quick to prepare
– perfect if friends turn up unexpectedly. Just
throw something on the barbie and lunch is ready!"

Ingredients

4 large green apples (200g), unpeeled

2 cups (80g) finely shredded green cabbage

½ cup small fresh mint leaves

2 green onions, sliced thinly on the diagonal

⅔ cup (80ml) coleslaw dressing

Method

1 Cut apple into matchsticks. Place apple, cabbage, mint, onion and dressing in a large bowl, season to taste; toss gently to combine.

ASIAN-STYLE STICKY
PORK SPARE RIBS
(recipe on page 170)

THE *Main* *Event*

This is the first dish I select when deciding on a menu, which is why I refer to it as "the main event". Be sure to choose something you can easily master, so you can enjoy the accolades.

CRISP-SKINNED FISH WITH ROAST GARLIC SKORDALIA

SERVES

4

PREP + COOK TIME

1 HOUR
+ COOLING

Ingredients

4 x 200g white fish fillets, skin on

2 tablespoons plain flour

ROAST GARLIC SKORDALIA

2 medium bulbs garlic (140g), unpeeled

600g small potatoes

½ cup (125ml) milk, warmed

1 tablespoon finely grated lemon rind

½ cup (125ml) olive oil

½ cup (140g) greek-style yoghurt

¼ cup (60ml) lemon juice

ROSEMARY OIL

¼ cup (60ml) olive oil

4 cloves garlic, sliced thinly

2 tablespoons rosemary leaves

Method

1 Make roast garlic skordalia.
2 Make rosemary oil.
3 Pat fish dry with paper towel; season. Sprinkle skin of the fish with flour, rub in gently to cover skin completely; shake away excess flour.
4 Heat 1 tablespoon of the rosemary oil in a medium frying pan; cook fish, skin-side down, for 2 minutes or until skin is crisp. Turn fish; cook fish through.
5 Serve fish with skordalia and drizzled with rosemary oil.

ROAST GARLIC SKORDALIA
Preheat oven to 220°C/200°C fan-forced. Wrap garlic in foil; place on an oven tray with potatoes. Roast for 30 minutes or until garlic and potatoes are soft. Stand until cool enough to handle. Peel potatoes; place flesh in a medium bowl. Squeeze garlic from cloves, add to potato with half the warm milk and the rind. Mash garlic and potato until smooth. Gradually stir in olive oil, 1 tablespoon at a time. Stir in yoghurt and juice; season to taste. Just before serving, heat remaining milk in a medium saucepan; add skordalia, cook, stirring, until heated through.

ROSEMARY OIL
Heat oil, garlic and rosemary in a small saucepan over low heat until garlic begins to colour. Cool.

COOKING NOTE

There are many recipes for skordalia – the roasted garlic gives this one a beautiful sweet and subtle taste.

LOBSTER WITH LIME & HERBS

SERVES

6

PREP + COOK TIME

35 MINUTES
+ REFRIGERATION

Ingredients

6 uncooked medium lobster tails (2.5kg)

⅓ cup (80ml) olive oil

2 teaspoons finely grated lime rind

½ cup (125ml) lime juice

2 cloves garlic, crushed

2 tablespoons each coarsely chopped fresh coriander and flat-leaf parsley

6 limes, cut into cheeks

Method

1 Remove and discard the soft shell from underneath lobster tails to expose the flesh.

2 Combine oil, rind, juice, garlic and herbs in a large bowl; add lobster, season. Cover; refrigerate for 1 hour.

3 Drain lobster; reserve marinade.

4 Cook lobster on a heated oiled barbecue (or grill pan or grill) over medium-high heat until browned all over and cooked through, brushing lobster occasionally with reserved marinade during cooking. Serve with lime cheeks.

COOKING NOTES

Don't overcook the lobster or it will be dry.

Instead of lobster, you can substitute Balmain Bugs or Moreton Bay Bugs.

ROAST PORTUGUESE SPATCHCOCK WITH OLIVES & CAPERS

SERVES

4

PREP + COOK TIME

1 HOUR
10 MINUTES

"I attended a wonderful charity dinner many years ago to raise money for Mission Australia. On the night, top Sydney chefs contributed dishes – and this spatchcock recipe. Thanks to Tetsuya, it was a winner!"

Ingredients

4 x 500g spatchcocks

2 cups (500ml) dry white wine, approximately

⅓ cup (65g) salted capers, rinsed, drained

40 pitted black olives

6 cloves garlic, chopped finely

1 tablespoon chopped oregano

1 cup (250ml) olive oil

sea salt flakes and freshly ground white pepper

2 tablespoons chopped flat-leaf parsley

Method

1 Preheat oven to 200°C/180°C fan-forced.

2 Place spatchcocks, breast-sides down, on a board. Cut through backbones with kitchen scissors. Turn the spatchcocks over; cut along breastbones with scissors. Place the spatchcock halves, skin-side up, in a deep baking dish. Season well.

3 Pour the wine into the dish until the liquid reaches halfway up the sides of the spatchcock. Add a little water if more liquid is required.

4 Scatter the capers, olives, garlic and oregano over the spatchcocks, then drizzle with the oil. Season with salt and white pepper. Bake for 45 minutes or until the skin is golden and the spatchcocks are cooked.

5 To serve, place spatchcocks in the centre of serving plates. Spoon a little of the pan juices over the top. Sprinkle with parsley. Serve with boiled chat potatoes, if you like.

ITALIAN PAN-FRIED LAMB FILLETS WITH SALSA VERDE

SERVES

4

PREP + COOK TIME

25 MINUTES
+ STANDING

"This is one of my favourite dishes for a casual lunch or when friends pop in. I have a soft spot for lamb tenderloins and find them more tender than back straps. They literally take only minutes to cook but have serious flavour."

Ingredients

2 tablespoons chopped rosemary

4 cloves garlic, crushed

2 tablespoons extra virgin olive oil

½ cup (125ml) lemon juice

1 tablespoon finely grated lemon zest

900g lamb fillets

150g mixed salad leaves

SALSA VERDE

1 cup coarsely chopped mint

1 cup coarsely chopped basil

1 cup coarsely chopped coriander

1 eschalot (25g), chopped finely

1 tablespoon rinsed, drained capers, finely chopped

8 pitted kalamata olives, finely chopped

2 tablespoons lemon juice

2 tablespoons extra virgin olive oil

Method

1 Combine rosemary, garlic, oil, juice and zest in a large bowl. Add lamb; toss to coat in marinade. Cover; stand for 1 hour.

2 Make salsa verde.

3 Preheat a barbecue (or grill pan or grill) to medium-high. Remove lamb from the marinade, draining well. Cook lamb for 3 minutes each side or until cooked to your liking. Remove from heat, cover loosely with foil; stand for 5 minutes before slicing.

4 Serve lamb topped with salsa verde, accompanied with salad leaves.

SALSA VERDE
Combine the ingredients in a medium bowl; season to taste.

COOKING NOTES

I often head to the farmers' markets to buy the lamb fresh from the farmers.

Be sure to rest the fillets for a few minutes before serving.

BARBECUED WHOLE SNAPPER WITH LIME & CHILLI DRESSING

SERVES

4

PREP + COOK TIME

50 MINUTES

Ingredients

1.5kg whole snapper, cleaned

1 stick fresh lemongrass (20g), bruised, cut into 5cm lengths

4 cloves garlic, crushed

6 kaffir lime leaves, torn

½ cup loosely packed coriander leaves

2 green onions, sliced thinly

1 lime, cut into wedges

LIME & CHILLI DRESSING

½ cup (125ml) sweet chilli sauce

½ cup (125ml) lime juice

2 teaspoons caster sugar

⅓ cup (80ml) light soy sauce

3cm piece fresh ginger (15g), grated finely

2 tablespoons fish sauce

2 tablespoons peanut oil

¼ cup finely chopped coriander

Method

1 Preheat a covered barbecue to medium-high with the hood closed. Once it reaches high heat, switch off the inside burner(s) where the fish parcel will sit, so that the heat is not directly under the fish.

2 Rinse fish inside and out; pat dry with paper towel. Make three shallow cuts, 1cm deep, in the thickest part of each side of fish.

3 Place a large sheet of baking paper on top of a large piece of foil. Place the fish in the centre of the baking paper; push the lemongrass, garlic and lime leaves into the fish cavity. Season fish. Fold over the baking paper and foil to enclose the fish, scrunching edges to seal. Place the wrapped fish on the barbecue and cook with the hood closed for 30 minutes, turning halfway, or until cooked through.

4 Make lime and chilli dressing.

5 Unwrap fish and carefully transfer to a serving plate. Pour dressing over fish; sprinkle with coriander leaves and onion. Serve with lime wedges.

LIME & CHILLI DRESSING

Combine the ingredients in a screw-top jar. Shake well.

CHICKEN PIECES WITH PROSCIUTTO & ROSEMARY

SERVES

8

PREP + COOK TIME

1 HOUR
+ REFRIGERATION
& STANDING

"These juicy chicken pieces are flavoured with the essence of the Mediterranean – what a way to share a lazy weekend lunch with friends! The combination of fresh rosemary, zesty lemon and crunchy prosciutto is the perfect combination. This is also easy to prepare for a crowd."

Ingredients

10 free-range chicken marylands, divided into thighs & drumsticks

1 tablespoon lemon zest

¼ cup (60ml) lemon juice

⅓ cup finely chopped rosemary

½ cup (125ml) extra virgin olive oil

12 thin slices prosciutto (180g)

Method

1 Place the chicken pieces in one large or two medium shallow baking dishes. Add the zest, juice, rosemary and oil; toss to coat the chicken. Turn the chicken skin-side up. Season with freshly ground black pepper. Refrigerate the chicken for at least 1 hour.

2 Preheat oven to 230°C/210°C fan-forced. Bake the chicken for 25 minutes. If using two dishes, swap their positions halfway through cooking. Check that the chicken is cooked by inserting a skewer into the thickest part of the thigh. If the juices run pink, return the chicken to the oven for 5–10 minutes or until the juices run clear. Cover with foil; stand for 15 minutes.

3 Meanwhile, place the prosciutto slices on an oven tray in a single layer. Bake for 5-10 minutes or until crisp. Place the prosciutto on top of the chicken to serve.

serving suggestion Serve with a salad and fresh crusty bread.

COOKING NOTE

If you'd like to serve a sauce with this, add ½ cup (125ml) hot chicken stock and ¼ cup (60ml) verjuice to the baking dish while the chicken is resting.

JAMES'S OVEN ROASTED RACK OF LAMB

SERVES

4

PREP + COOK TIME

50 MINUTES

"A good friend of mine, James Vaile – who doesn't rate himself in the kitchen – whipped up this rack of lamb one night and I thought it was pure magic. The crunchy rosemary parmesan crust is to die for!"

Ingredients

⅓ cup (80ml) olive oil

750g chat or kipfler potatoes, peeled, cut into wedges

2 x 8-cutlet racks of lamb, french-trimmed

¼ cup (70g) dijon mustard

1 handful chopped rosemary

3 cloves garlic, chopped

½ cup (35g) panko breadcrumbs

¾ cup (60g) finely grated parmesan

Method

1 Preheat oven to 200°C/180°C fan-forced.

2 Place 1 tablespoon of the oil in a medium baking dish; add potatoes and toss to coat. Season well. Roast for 10 minutes.

3 Meanwhile, heat another 1 tablespoon of the oil in a medium frying pan over medium-high heat. Add the lamb; cook for 3 minutes or until golden brown on both sides. Season the lamb, then spread mustard over lamb.

4 Combine the rosemary, garlic, breadcrumbs, remaining olive oil and parmesan in a large bowl.

5 Top the lamb evenly with the breadcrumb mixture to create a crust, pressing the crust on gently. Transfer to the baking dish with potatoes, bone-side down. Roast for 20 minutes.

6 Cover lamb and potatoes loosely with foil; stand for 5 minutes. Slice the racks in half and serve immediately with the roasted potatoes.

serving suggestion Serve with buttered steamed green beans.

SPAGHETTI WITH PRAWNS, CHILLI & LEMON

SERVES	PREP + COOK TIME
4	25 MINUTES

"This dish is so easy to pull together and tastes sensational. The flavours of the garlic, chilli, prawns and lemon zest just jump out at you!"

Ingredients

400g spaghetti

¼ cup (60ml) olive oil

3 cloves garlic, chopped finely

2 fresh red chillies, seeded, chopped finely

2 large tomatoes (440g), peeled, chopped

¼ cup (60ml) fish or chicken stock

1 teaspoon finely grated lemon zest

2 tablespoons lemon juice

400g medium green tiger prawns, peeled

100g baby rocket or kale leaves

Method

1 Cook the spaghetti in a large saucepan of boiling well-salted water until just tender; drain.

2 Meanwhile, heat the oil in a large, deep frying pan over medium-high heat. Add the garlic and chilli; cook for 1 minute. Add the tomato and stock; cook for a further minute. Add the zest, juice and prawns; cook for 4 minutes or until prawns are just cooked through. Season to taste.

3 Add the spaghetti and rocket to the pan; toss well. Divide among four warmed plates or pasta bowls and serve.

SUMMER PENNE WITH ZUCCHINI, CHILLI & FETTA

"Once you've had this, you'll be back for more. There's something so refreshing about the zesty lemon and the crunch of the zucchini."

Ingredients

500g penne pasta

½ cup (125ml) extra virgin olive oil

4 cloves garlic, chopped

2 small fresh red chillies, chopped

4 medium zucchinis (480g), grated coarsely

3 teaspoons finely grated lemon rind

50g butter

250g fetta, crumbled

1¼ cups (100g) finely grated parmesan

Method

1 Cook the penne in a large saucepan of boiling well-salted water until just tender; drain, cover to keep warm.

2 Heat oil in the same saucepan over medium heat. Add the garlic, chilli, zucchini and rind. Cook gently for 1-2 minutes or until softened but not browned.

3 Return the hot pasta to the saucepan with the butter and fetta. Toss together and season to taste. Serve topped with parmesan.

COOKING NOTE

Remove the seeds from the chillies for a milder flavour.

MAGGIE'S CHICKEN CURRY

SERVES

6

PREP + COOK TIME

1 HOUR
30 MINUTES

"Maggie Tabberer was fashion editor on The Australian Women's Weekly before me. She had a fabulous farmhouse in the NSW Southern Highlands and invited friends for country weekends. This was one of her signature dishes."

Ingredients

5 cloves garlic, chopped

2cm piece fresh ginger (15g), grated

¼ cup (60ml) extra virgin olive oil

1.2kg chicken breast fillets or thigh fillets, cut into bite-sized pieces

2 medium brown onions (300g), chopped coarsely

4 small fresh red chillies, chopped finely

1 bunch mint, chopped

2 lemongrass stalks, chopped

1 bunch coriander, chopped

2 tablespoons thai green curry paste

1 medium lemon (140g), peeled, chopped finely

2 x 400ml cans coconut milk

2 teaspoons sambal oelek

1 tablespoon mango chutney

2 medium ripe tomatoes (300g), chopped

100g unsalted cashews

2 tablespoons chopped coriander, extra

Method

1 Blend the garlic and ginger with a little water into a paste.

2 Heat some of the oil in a large heavy frying pan over high heat. Cook the chicken, in batches, with more oil as needed, until browned lightly all over. Transfer chicken to a large bowl.

3 Add a little more of the oil to the same pan. Add the onion and chilli; cook, stirring, over medium heat for 10 minutes or until onion is soft. Add the garlic mixture and stir well.

4 Return the chicken to the pan with the remaining ingredients, except the cashews and extra coriander. Cook, covered, over very low heat for 1 hour, stirring occasionally.

5 Toast the cashews in a small dry frying pan until browned lightly and fragrant.

6 Serve the curry in large bowls, sprinkled with cashews, extra coriander and steamed jasmine rice, if you like.

MEDITERRANEAN CHICKEN

SERVES	PREP + COOK TIME
8	1 HOUR

"Crispy, juicy and full of flavour, this is the dish my friends rave about! I serve it from the roasting pan I cook it in, straight from the oven to the table. Perfect for a relaxed crowd, and such an easy and inexpensive dish."

Ingredients

800g chat potatoes, halved if large

8 chicken thighs on the bone, skin on

3 teaspoons sweet paprika

2 medium red onions (340g), peeled, quartered

2 small red capsicums (300g), cut into strips

1 medium yellow capsicum (200g), cut into strips

4 cloves garlic, crushed

¼ cup (60ml) olive oil

1 tablespoon chopped oregano

400g can diced tomatoes

20 pitted black olives

150g crumbled fetta

2 tablespoons chopped flat-leaf parsley

Method

1 Preheat oven to 200°C/180°C fan-forced.

2 Place potatoes in a large saucepan of water and bring to the boil. Boil for 5 minutes; drain.

3 Dry chicken pieces with paper towel and trim any excess fat. Place the chicken in a large baking dish; sprinkle with paprika, rubbing in all over the chicken pieces.

4 Add the onion, capsicum, garlic and potatoes. Pour oil over vegetables, sprinkle with the oregano; season well. Bake for 30 minutes.

5 Add the tomato and olives; bake for a further 15 minutes or until chicken is cooked through.

6 Sprinkle fetta and parsley over the chicken; serve immediately.

ASIAN-STYLE STICKY PORK SPARE RIBS

SERVES 4

PREP + COOK TIME

1 HOUR 15 MINUTES + COOLING & REFRIGERATION

"This Asian take on American pork ribs takes lip-smacking flavour to a whole new level. I serve these on a platter in the centre of the table and let everyone go for it. Definitely not the night for the good tablecloth!"

Ingredients

10 cloves garlic, crushed

2 fresh long red chillies, chopped finely

1 cup (250ml) kecap manis

1 cup (250ml) light soy sauce

⅓ cup (80ml) fish sauce

¾ cup (165g) firmly packed brown sugar

½ cup (125ml) chicken stock

6 star anise

2kg pork spare ribs, cut chinese-style (see note)

1 tablespoon sesame seeds, toasted

1 long green chilli, sliced

lime cheeks, to serve

Method

1 Combine garlic, red chilli, sauces, sugar, stock and star anise in a large saucepan; bring to the boil. Remove from heat, transfer to a large bowl; cool.

2 Add ribs to marinade, turning to coat. Cover; refrigerate for 3 hours or overnight.

3 Preheat oven to 210°C/190°C fan-forced. Transfer ribs and marinade to a large baking dish, cover with foil or a lid; roast for 30 minutes. Uncover dish; turn ribs and baste with marinade. Roast for a further 30 minutes or until caramelised and sticky.

4 Sprinkle ribs with sesame seeds and green chilli. Serve with lime cheeks.

serving suggestion Accompany with steamed jasmine rice and steamed Asian greens.

COOKING NOTE

In Chinese cuisine, the ribs are generally cut into 7-10cm lengths before cooking. Ask your butcher to do this for you.

NOUGAT
SEMIFREDDO
WITH ORANGE
& HONEY SYRUP
(recipe on page 192)

SOMETHING *Sweet*

For me, desserts should possess the WOW factor, since it'll be the last thing your guests will remember about the meal. This is your chance to shine.

CHOCOLATE TART WITH SUMMER BERRIES

SERVES

10

PREP + COOK TIME

1 HOUR
+ COOLING

"I don't consider myself an outstanding cook – rather, I like to whip up dishes with a knockout factor but a low degree of difficulty. This cake fits the brief. It has a flourless chocolate base, so when it cools, it collapses a little in the middle... don't panic! It looks and tastes amazing because you just fill it with fresh berries, then shake icing sugar on top."

Ingredients

200g dark cooking chocolate, chopped coarsely

200g unsalted butter, chopped coarsely

4 eggs, separated

1 cup (220g) caster sugar

2 tablespoons icing sugar, sifted

2 cups (260g) fresh mixed berries (such as strawberries, blueberries, raspberries, mulberries, blackberries)

Method

1 Preheat oven to 180°C/160°C fan-forced. Grease and line base and side of a deep 24cm round springform cake tin or the base of a deep 24cm round loose-based fluted flan tin with baking paper.

2 Place the chocolate and butter in a medium saucepan over very low heat; stir until just melted and smooth (take care it doesn't burn). Cool.

3 Beat egg yolks and half the sugar in a small bowl with an electric mixer until thick, pale and creamy. Add the chocolate mixture; mix until well combined.

4 Beat egg whites in a small clean bowl with an electric mixer until soft peaks form. Gradually add the remaining sugar, a tablespoon at a time, beating until sugar dissolves between additions; beat until mixture is thick and shiny. Gently fold egg whites into the chocolate mixture, in two batches.

5 Pour mixture into prepared tin. Bake for 35 minutes or until a skewer inserted into the centre comes out clean. Cool tart in tin. (The centre of the tart may sink a little.)

6 Carefully remove tart from tin; remove lining paper. Dust the tart with half the icing sugar. Top with berries and dust with remaining icing sugar. Serve immediately.

CHOCOLATE PANETTONE PUDDING

SERVES

8

PREP + COOK TIME

45 MINUTES
+ STANDING

"The moment it comes out of the oven, this ridiculously naughty pudding looks sensational. I like to let it sit for an hour before baking because the more liquid it absorbs, the fluffier it will be."

Ingredients

800g plain panettone

⅔ cup (220g) blackberry jam

2½ cups (600g) ricotta

½ cup (100g) dark chocolate, chopped

5 eggs

2 cups (500ml) milk

200ml thick cream

1 tablespoon vanilla bean paste

¼ cup (55g) raw sugar

Method

1 Preheat oven to 200°C/180°C fan-forced. Lightly grease a 2.5-litre (10-cup) ovenproof dish.
2 Cut panettone in half, then cut each piece into 2.5cm-thick slices.
3 Spread a generous layer of jam over the panettone slices. Arrange the panettone in overlapping rows with slices of ricotta in between. Scatter with chocolate.
4 Lightly whisk eggs, milk, cream and vanilla bean paste in a large bowl until combined. Pour mixture over the panettone. Stand for 30 minutes to 1 hour. Sprinkle with sugar.

5 Cover pudding with a sheet of baking paper, then a sheet of foil, folding around the dish to seal. Bake pudding for 25 minutes. Remove foil and baking paper. Increase the oven temperature to 220°C/200°C fan-forced. Bake the pudding for a further 10 minutes or until slightly crisp, puffed and cooked through.
6 Serve warm.

serving suggestion Serve pudding with vanilla bean ice-cream or crème fraîche.

RASPBERRY ALMOND CRUMBLE TART

SERVES

8

PREP + COOK TIME

1 HOUR
+ REFRIGERATION
& COOLING

Ingredients

1½ cups (225g) frozen raspberries

1 teaspoon icing sugar

ALMOND CRUMBLE PLASTRY

150g butter, softened

1 teaspoon vanilla extract

⅔ cup (150g) caster sugar

1 egg

½ cup (60g) almond meal

1½ cups (225g) plain flour

Method

1 Make almond crumble pastry.
2 Roll two-thirds of the pastry between sheets of baking paper until large enough to line an 11cm x 35cm rectangular loose-based flan tin. Lift pastry into tin, press into base and sides; trim edge. Prick pastry base with a fork; refrigerate for 30 minutes. Reserve remaining pastry.
3 Meanwhile, preheat oven to 200°C/180°C fan-forced.
4 Place the tin on an oven tray; bake tart for 10 minutes or until browned lightly.
5 Sprinkle raspberries over the pastry base; sprinkle with remaining crumbled pastry. Bake for a further 20 minutes or until well browned; cool in pan.
6 Dust with sifted icing sugar before serving.

ALMOND CRUMBLE PASTRY
Beat butter in a small bowl with an electric mixer until smooth. Add extract, sugar and egg; beat until combined. Stir in almond meal and half the flour. Using your hand, work in remaining flour. Knead pastry on a floured surface until smooth. Wrap the pastry in plastic wrap; refrigerate for 30 minutes.

serving suggestion Serve with double-thick cream, ice-cream or custard.

COOKING NOTE

This recipe is best made on the day of serving, as the raspberries will soften the pastry.

EASIEST BANANA SOUFFLÉS

SERVES	PREP + COOK TIME
4	25 MINUTES

"Compliments of chef Greg Doyle, this is the easiest soufflé recipe that you'll ever come across. Not only that, it tastes unbelievably good!"

Ingredients

20g unsalted butter, melted

¼ cup (55g) white sugar

2 medium ripe bananas (400g), chopped coarsely

2 teaspoons honey

4 egg whites

1 tablespoon caster sugar

2 teaspoons icing sugar

Method

1 Preheat oven to 200°C/180°C fan-forced. Using the melted butter, grease 4 x ¾-cup (180ml) ramekins. Sprinkle insides of dishes evenly with white sugar; shake away excess. Place dishes on an oven tray.

2 Blend or process banana and honey on high until the mixture forms a smooth paste. Transfer to a large bowl.

3 Beat egg whites in a small bowl with an electric mixer until just before soft peaks form. Sprinkle with caster sugar; beat until soft peaks form. (Don't over-beat the egg whites or the soufflés will be dry.) Fold egg mixture into banana mixture, in three batches.

4 Spoon mixture among dishes; tap ramekins gently on the bench to release any air bubbles. Using a palette knife, scrape off any excess mix from the top of the dishes. Wipe the inside of the rim with your finger to help make the soufflé rise evenly.

5 Bake for 7-8 minutes. The soufflés should be soft – not fully cooked in the centre. Dust with icing sugar and serve immediately.

CLOVE PANNA COTTA WITH FRESH FIGS

SERVES

4

PREP + COOK TIME

30 MINUTES
+ STANDING
& COOLING
& REFRIGERATION

"A magnificent fruit, figs have their origin in the long, hot summers of the eastern Mediterranean. As well as eaten fresh, they also taste exquisite sprinkled with cinnamon and demerara sugar and grilled for dessert."

Ingredients

1 teaspoon whole cloves

300ml thickened cream

⅔ cup (160ml) milk

2 teaspoons gelatine

2 tablespoons caster sugar

½ teaspoon vanilla extract

4 medium fresh figs (240g)

2 tablespoons honey

Method

1 Grease 4 x ½-cup (125ml) moulds.

2 Place cloves, cream and milk in a small saucepan; stand for 10 minutes. Sprinkle gelatine and sugar over cream mixture; stir over low heat, without boiling, until gelatine and sugar dissolve. Stir in extract. Strain into a medium jug; cool to room temperature.

3 Divide the mixture among prepared moulds, cover; refrigerate for 3 hours or until set.

4 Quarter figs; heat honey in a small saucepan over low heat, stirring, until warm.

5 Turn panna cotta onto serving plates; serve with figs, drizzled with honey.

RHUBARB SPONGE PUDDINGS

MAKES

8

PREP + COOK TIME

1 HOUR

Ingredients

5 cups (700g) coarsely chopped, trimmed rhubarb

2 tablespoons caster sugar

2 tablespoons orange juice

500g strawberries, sliced thinly

SPONGE MIXTURE

2 eggs

½ cup (110g) caster sugar

½ cup (75g) self-raising flour

½ tablespoon cornflour

Method

1 Preheat oven to 180°C/160°C fan-forced.

2 Cook rhubarb, sugar and juice in a large saucepan over low heat, stirring, until sugar dissolves. Cook, uncovered, for 10 minutes or until rhubarb is tender. Stir in the strawberries.

3 Meanwhile, make sponge mixture.

4 Spoon the fruit mixture into 8 x 1-cup (250ml) ovenproof dishes; bake for 5 minutes or until fruit mixture is bubbling hot.

5 Top hot rhubarb mixture evenly with sponge mixture; bake for 30 minutes. Serve immediately.

SPONGE MIXTURE Beat eggs in a small bowl with an electric mixer for 10 minutes or until thick and creamy. Gradually add sugar, beating until sugar dissolves. Fold triple-sifted flour and cornflour into egg mixture.

serving suggestion Serve with custard or cream.

COOKING NOTE

You need about 10 stems of rhubarb for this recipe.

STRAWBERRY & RHUBARB DESSERT

SERVES

4

PREP + COOK TIME

30 MINUTES
+ COOLING

"I'm a bit of a fan of fruity desserts – they're simple, elegant and always leave the palate refreshed. Rhubarb and strawberry are a wonderful combination, and the crumbly topping of coconut and almonds adds a lovely texture to this delightful dessert."

Ingredients

500g rhubarb, cut into 2cm pieces

⅓ cup (75g) caster sugar

2 teaspoons finely grated orange zest

⅓ cup (80ml) orange juice, approximately

250g strawberries, quartered

1 tablespoon grand marnier

½ cup (80g) currants

½ cup (40g) shredded coconut

½ cup (75g) finely chopped roasted blanched almonds

1 cup (280g) greek-style yoghurt

small mint leaves, to garnish

Method

1 Preheat oven to 180°C/160°C fan-forced.

2 Combine rhubarb, sugar, zest and juice in a large ceramic baking dish. Cover dish with foil; bake for 15 minutes. Remove the foil, add strawberries to dish; bake for a further 5 minutes or until fruit is tender. Remove dish from oven; stir in Grand Marnier. Cool.

3 Combine currants, coconut and almonds in a medium bowl.

4 Spoon rhubarb mixture evenly into 4 x 1-cup serving glasses. Top with yoghurt, then currant mixture and mint.

COOKING NOTES

You'll need 1 bunch of rhubarb and the rind and juice from 1 medium orange for this recipe.

Prepare the rhubarb in advance and chill. Combine ingredients at the last moment.

ORANGE ICE-CREAM WITH CINNAMON SYRUP

SERVES

6

PREP + COOK TIME

30 MINUTES
+ FREEZING

"When you're searching for a really refreshing finish to your meal, it doesn't get much better than this. The perfect summer dessert, this ice-cream looks beautiful and is a personal favourite because it's so simple and elegant. Best of all, it's easily made the day before."

Ingredients

¾ cup (250g) good-quality orange marmalade

2 litres (8 cups) good-quality vanilla ice-cream, softened at room temperature

½ cup (125ml) water

½ cup (110g) caster sugar

⅓ cup (80ml) orange juice

2 teaspoons finely grated orange zest

2 cinnamon sticks

2 tablespoons orange blossom water

1 medium orange (240g), segmented

1 tablespoon slivered pistachios

2 tablespoons small mint leaves

Method

1 Line a 2-litre (8-cup) terrine mould or loaf pan with plastic wrap, extending plastic 10cm over sides.

2 Reserve 2 tablespoons of the marmalade. Place the remaining marmalade in a large bowl with the ice-cream; stir until well combined. Spoon mixture into prepared mould or pan; smooth surface. Cover with the overhanging plastic wrap. Freeze overnight or until firm.

3 Meanwhile, combine the water, sugar, juice and reserved marmalade in a small saucepan over low heat; stir until sugar is dissolved. Add the zest, cinnamon and orange blossom water; simmer, uncovered, for 3-4 minutes or until syrup is thickened slightly. Discard cinnamon. Cool; refrigerate until chilled.

4 To serve, carefully turn the ice-cream from the mould onto a serving platter, remove lining plastic. Cut ice-cream into thick slices. Drizzle with the cinnamon syrup and top with orange segments, nuts and mint.

NOUGAT SEMIFREDDO WITH ORANGE & HONEY SYRUP

SERVES 4

PREP + COOK TIME

25 MINUTES
+ FREEZING
& STANDING

Ingredients

1 vanilla bean

3 eggs, separated

⅓ cup (75g) caster sugar

1½ cups (375ml) thickened cream

200g nougat, chopped finely

½ cup (75g) coarsely chopped, roasted, shelled pistachios

1 tablespoon honey

ORANGE HONEY SYRUP

¼ cup (90g) honey

1 tablespoon finely grated orange rind

2 tablespoons orange juice

Method

1 Split vanilla bean in half lengthways; scrape seeds into a small bowl (reserve pod for another use). Add yolks and sugar to bowl; beat with an electric mixer until thick and creamy. Transfer mixture to a large bowl.

2 Beat cream in a small bowl with an electric mixer until soft peaks form; gently fold cream into the yolk mixture.

3 Beat egg whites in a separate clean small bowl with an electric mixer until soft peaks form. Gently fold half the egg whites into cream mixture; fold in nougat, nuts, honey and remaining egg whites. Spoon mixture into a loaf pan lined with baking paper or foil, or a stainless steel bowl. Cover with foil; freeze for 3 hours or until just firm.

4 Make orange honey syrup.

5 Stand semifreddo at room temperature for 10 minutes before serving with syrup.

ORANGE HONEY SYRUP Bring ingredients to the boil in a small saucepan. Reduce heat; simmer, uncovered, for 2 minutes.

COOKING NOTES

A traditional Italian dessert, semifreddo loosely translates as "a bit cold", and can refer to any partially frozen sweet served at the end of a meal.

Using the actual vanilla bean imparts the real taste of aromatic vanilla to a recipe.

Use a lined loaf pan if you wish to turn the semifreddo out and slice it for serving; otherwise, scoop it from the bowl.

STRAWBERRY YOGHURT BRÛLÉE

SERVES

4

PREP + COOK TIME

15 MINUTES

"Now we're talking big bang for little bucks! This is quick and easy, with a bit of show to impress your guests – you just need to buy a small blowtorch from a kitchen shop. With fresh strawberries, some yoghurt and a crunchy caramelised sugar topping, this is seriously special."

Ingredients

250g strawberries
2 cups (560g) greek-style yoghurt
½ cup (110g) white sugar

Method

1 Finely slice 4 of the strawberries (6, if small); coarsely chop the remaining strawberries.
2 Combine yoghurt, the chopped strawberries and 1 tablespoon of the sugar in a large bowl.
3 Divide yoghurt mixture among four ¾-cup (180ml) ovenproof cups. Top with strawberry slices. Sprinkle evenly with the remaining sugar (about 1 tablespoon each).
4 Pass the flame of a kitchen blowtorch over the sugar until it is melted and caramelised (about 30 seconds). Serve immediately.

Cheese PLATTERS

Whether or not you're having sweet desserts, consider serving an elegant cheese platter with a varied selection of cow's, goat's and blue cheeses served with dried muscatels, fresh fruit, quince paste and crunchy bread.

Select cheeses with varying tastes and textures. A good selection is a smooth punchy cheese like marinated goat's cheese, a soft buttery ripened Brie or Taleggio, a hard cheese like Gruyère or Manchego and a more pungent blue cheese like Roquefort or Stilton. Accompany with crackers and crostini twists or, for a nice touch, tear bite-sized chunks from the centre of a fresh loaf of bread and toast in the oven for a few minutes with a good splash of olive oil and a little sea salt. Add sweet complements like crunchy, fresh pear, grapes, dried figs, walnuts, honey and jam. Serve it all up at room temperature on wooden cutting boards or big white platters with a couple of cheese knives. If you want to dress things up, include handwritten labels with the cheeses.

Special
OCCASIONS

A little imagination goes a long way to creating a wonderful experience for your guests.

CHINESE NEW YEAR

This is your big chance to show off your cooking skills with a wok, or order in your favourite Chinese takeaway. Brighten your dining table with a red cloth and gold silks, set out oriental ornaments and throw around opulent cushions. Serve lychee martinis, jasmine tea and fortune cookies.

Birthdays

Get creative with themes, menus and the birthday cake. Keep it simple or go all-out with banners, giant or confetti-filled balloons, paper lanterns, flowers, streamers or fairy lights... the more the merrier.

Valentine's Day

INDULGE IN AMOROUS TASTE SENSATIONS LIKE OYSTERS, CHAMPAGNE AND CHOCOLATE – AND PLAY A LITTLE BOSSA NOVA OR SOME CORNY LOVE BALLADS!

CHRISTMAS

Festive must-haves start with the tree and sparkling decorations. I like to celebrate the festive season with alfresco lunches and seafood barbecues on balmy nights. Track down some cool Christmas lounge music and consider doing a Kris Kringle gift exchange.

EASTER gives us a few days to kick back and indulge in fresh seafood and sparkling wines before tucking into chocolate treats for dessert. An Easter egg hunt after lunch is good fun for grown-ups and kids.

FRUIT CAKE
CREAM PARFAITS
(recipe on page 227)

Festive

FAVOURITES

It's the end of the year, so go all out… set a wonderful table, create the ultimate festive menu, chill the drinks and share this time with those you love.

BLOODY MARY

SERVES	PREP TIME
1	5 MINUTES

Enjoyed by American author and journalist Ernest Hemingway, this potent pick-me-up packs a tangy punch for holiday brunches.

Ingredients

30ml vodka, chilled

60ml tomato juice, chilled

1 tablespoon fresh lemon juice

splash of worcestershire sauce

pinch of sugar

pinch of celery salt

pinch of black pepper

dash of tabasco sauce

ice-cubes

1 stalk celery

Method

1 Combine vodka, tomato juice and lemon juice in a jug.

2 Add Worcestershire sauce, sugar, celery salt, black pepper and Tabasco sauce. Stir.

3 Add ice-cubes to a highball glass. Pour vodka mixture over ice. Garnish with celery.

PEA, MINT & ALMOND SALAD WITH MUSTARD & CIDER DRESSING

SERVES 6

PREP + COOK TIME

30 MINUTES

"Peas are one of my favourite vegetables and in this recipe four varieties are used. The mint adds a lovely freshness and the nuts a crunchy finish."

Ingredients

150g snow peas, trimmed

150g sugar snap peas, trimmed

125g snow pea sprouts, trimmed (see note)

150g young pea tendrils, trimmed (see note)

1 cup loosely packed mint leaves

½ cup (70g) slivered almonds, roasted

MUSTARD & CIDER DRESSING

2 tablespoons olive oil

1 tablespoon cider vinegar

2 teaspoons wholegrain mustard

Method

1 Cook snow peas and sugar snap peas in a medium saucepan of boiling salted water for 2 minutes or until barely tender; drain. Rinse under cold running water; drain.
2 Make mustard & cider dressing.
3 Place peas in a large bowl with sprouts, tendrils, mint, nuts and dressing; toss gently to combine.

MUSTARD & CIDER DRESSING
Combine ingredients in a small bowl; season to taste.

COOKING NOTE

Snow pea sprouts and pea tendrils can sometimes be hard to get. You can use bean sprouts or any other type of sprouts instead.

RUBY GRAPEFRUIT & POMEGRANATE SALAD

SERVES

4

PREP + COOK TIME

15 MINUTES

Ingredients

3 ruby red grapefruit (1kg)

¼ cup (60ml) olive oil

2 tablespoons coarsely chopped fresh chervil

100g curly endive leaves

½ cup (125ml) pomegranate seeds (see note)

½ cup (55g) coarsely chopped walnuts, roasted

Method

1 Juice half of one grapefruit; reserve juice. Peel remaining grapefruit; slice thickly.

2 Place the reserved juice in a screw-top jar with oil and chervil, season to taste; shake well.

3 Place endive in a large bowl with dressing; toss gently tc combine. Season to taste.

4 Arrange endive, grapefruit and pomegranate on a serving plate; sprinkle with nuts.

COOKING NOTE

Cut a whole pomegranate in half and scrape the seeds from flesh with your fingers while holding the pomegranate upside down in a bowl of cold water. The seeds will sink and the white pith will float.

HOT-SMOKED TROUT WITH COCONUT & PEANUT NAM JIM

SERVES

24

PREP + COOK TIME

40 MINUTES

Ingredients

1 medium pomelo (680g), segmented

200g flaked hot-smoked trout

100g coconut flesh, sliced thinly

1 cup each loosely packed small fresh thai basil and coriander leaves

24 betel leaves (see notes)

¼ cup (35g) crushed roasted peanuts

¼ cup (50g) salmon roe

PEANUT NAM JIM
¼ cup (35g) roasted unsalted peanuts

¼ cup (65g) grated palm sugar

¼ cup (60ml) fish sauce

1 fresh small green chilli, chopped finely

1cm piece fresh ginger (5g), grated finely

1 teaspoon finely grated lime rind

¼ cup (60ml) lime juice

1 tablespoon reserved coconut liquid (see notes)

Method

1 Make peanut nam jim.

2 Break the pomelo segments into small pieces; place in a large bowl. Add the trout, coconut and three-quarters of the combined herbs.

3 Place betel leaves on a serving platter; top with trout mixture. Drizzle with peanut nam jim, then sprinkle with remaining herbs, peanuts and salmon roe.

PEANUT NAM JIM Lightly grease an oven tray; sprinkle peanuts onto tray. Heat sugar and 2 teaspoons of the fish sauce in a small saucepan; cook for 2 minutes or until lightly caramelised. Pour over peanuts; cool until set, then break into pieces. Using a mortar and pestle (or blender or food processor) pound pieces into a fine powder. Place in a small bowl; stir in remaining ingredients.

COOKING NOTES

Betel leaves are available from most Asian food stores and some greengrocers.

To open a fresh coconut, pierce one of the "eyes", then drain the liquid. Reserve for the peanut nam jim.

To easily remove flesh from coconut, roast coconut briefly in a very hot oven until cracks appear in the shell. Cool, then break the coconut apart. Use a metal spoon to remove the flesh.

BUTTERFLIED LAMB WITH MINT SAUCE

SERVES

10

PREP + COOK TIME

40 MINUTES
+ REFRIGERATION
& STANDING

Ingredients

½ cup (90g) honey

1 tablespoon wholegrain mustard

2kg butterflied leg of lamb

¼ cup loosely packed fresh rosemary sprigs

MINT SAUCE

½ cup (110g) firmly packed brown sugar

½ cup (125ml) water

1½ cups (375ml) cider vinegar

½ cup finely chopped fresh mint

Method

1 Make mint sauce.

2 Combine a quarter of the mint sauce, the honey and mustard in a large shallow dish; add lamb, turn to coat in marinade. Cover; refrigerate for 3 hours or overnight, turning occasionally. Refrigerate the remaining mint sauce, separately.

3 Drain lamb; place, fat-side down, on a heated, oiled grill plate (or grill or barbecue) over medium heat. Cover lamb loosely with foil; cook for 10 minutes or until browned underneath. Uncover; turn lamb, sprinkle with rosemary. Cook, covered, for 10 minutes or until cooked as desired (or cook by indirect heat in a covered barbecue following manufacturer's instructions). Remove from heat; stand, covered, for 15 minutes.

4 Slice lamb thinly; serve with remaining mint sauce.

MINT SAUCE Stir sugar and the water in a small saucepan over low heat until the sugar dissolves. Bring to the boil. Reduce heat; simmer, uncovered, without stirring, for 5 minutes or until syrup thickens slightly. Combine syrup, vinegar and mint in a small bowl.

serving suggestion Serve with baby potatoes and a tomato and radish salad.

COOKING NOTES

The mint sauce can be made several days ahead. Cover and refrigerate.

Ask the butcher to butterfly a leg of lamb for you.

BARBECUED ORANGE MARMALADE GLAZED HAM

SERVES

12

PREP + COOK TIME

2 HOURS
30 MINUTES

Ingredients

7kg cooked leg of ham

350g jar orange marmalade

¼ cup (55g) firmly packed brown sugar

¼ cup (60ml) orange juice

whole cloves, to decorate (optional)

1 sprig bay leaves, leaves removed

Method

1 Preheat a covered barbecue (to about 180°C.)

2 Cut through rind of ham 10cm from the shank end of the leg. To remove the rind, run thumb around edge of rind just under skin. Start pulling rind from widest edge of ham, then continue to pull rind carefully away from the fat up to the shank end. Remove rind completely. Score across the fat at about 3cm intervals, cutting lightly through the surface of the fat (not the meat) in a diamond pattern.

3 Stir marmalade, sugar and juice in a small saucepan over low heat until sugar dissolves.

4 Place ham in a large, deep, disposable baking dish. Brush ham well with marmalade glaze; cover shank end with foil.

5 Cook ham, in covered barbecue, using indirect heat, following manufacturer's instructions, for 40 minutes. Decorate ham with cloves (if using), brush ham with pan juices; cook for a further 40 minutes or until browned all over, brushing occasionally with marmalade glaze during cooking. Scatter with bay leaves for the final 15 minutes of cooking time.

COOKING NOTES

Cooking using indirect heat on a barbecue is the best way to barbecue large cuts or joints of meat. The interior heat circulates around the food, cooking it through without burning. The heat beads or coals are placed around the outside perimeter of the bottom grill, rather than burning directly under the food. Or, if using a gas burner or electric barbecue, the burners directly underneath the food are switched off, while the burners around the food are left on.

The ham can also be cooked in a preheated oven at 180°C/160° fan-forced for 1 hour 20 minutes, adding cloves (if using) halfway through cooking. Place the ham on an oiled wire rack over a large baking dish that has been double-lined with baking paper (this stops the glaze burning your dish, making the clean-up much easier.)

BAKED SALMON WITH HERB & WALNUT SALSA

SERVES

PREP + COOK TIME

50 MINUTES

For many years, I was fortunate to host *The Australian Women's Weekly*'s TV Christmas special. One year we featured chef Michael Moore and his very simple but elegant salmon dish – it's been a favourite for my Christmas table ever since.

Ingredients

1.3kg salmon fillet, skin on, pin-boned

¼ cup (60ml) extra virgin olive oil

1 handful flat-leaf parsley leaves, chopped coarsely

1 cup coarsely chopped dill

½ cup (50g) walnuts, roasted, chopped coarsely

1 clove garlic, crushed

2 tablespoons baby capers, rinsed, drained

3 teaspoons finely grated lemon rind

1 tablespoon lemon juice

extra virgin olive oil, extra

1 medium lemon (140g), cut into wedges

Method

1 Preheat oven to 200°C/180°C fan-forced. Line a large oven tray with baking paper.

2 Place the salmon, skin-side down, on oven tray and brush with 2 tablespoons of the oil. Season well. Cook salmon for 10–15 minutes or until cooked to your liking. It will continue to cook after it is taken out of the oven, so it should be removed from the oven slightly underdone.

3 Meanwhile, combine the remaining oil in a medium bowl with parsley, dill, nuts, garlic, capers, rind and juice.

4 Transfer the salmon to a serving platter; sprinkle with the herb and walnut mixture and drizzle with a little extra oil. Serve immediately with lemon wedges.

serving suggestion Serve with a garden salad.

SMOKY CHILLI CHICKEN WITH CRUSHED AVOCADO

SERVES

4-6

PREP + COOK TIME

1 HOUR +
REFRIGERATION

Every summer I discover a new recipe that becomes the hot "crowd" favourite. This one, from *Gourmet Traveller*, now sits in my top 10! Easy, tasty and everyone loved it.

Ingredients

⅓ cup (80ml) olive oil

¼ cup (60ml) lime juice

2 teaspoons ground pasilla chilli (see note)

1 teaspoon each ground cumin and ground coriander

1 clove garlic, chopped finely

10 skinless chicken thigh fillets (2.2kg), chopped coarsely

3 corn cobs (1.2kg), husks removed

2 medium tomatoes (300g), chopped coarsely

12 corn tortillas (300g)

1 lime, cut into wedges

¼ cup loosely packed coriander sprigs, to garnish

CRUSHED AVOCADO

2 medium avocados (500g), chopped coarsely

2 cloves garlic, chopped finely

1 fresh small red chilli, chopped finely

2 tablespoons olive oil

2 tablespoons lime juice

pinch of ground pasilla chilli

½ cup coarsely chopped coriander

Method

1 Combine 2 tablespoons of the oil, half the juice, the spices and garlic in a large bowl; season to taste. Add chicken, stir to coat in marinade; cover, refrigerate for 20 minutes.

2 Meanwhile, heat a barbecue (or grill plate or grill) over medium-high heat. Drizzle corn with 1 tablespoon of the remaining oil; cook, turning occasionally, for 10 minutes or until tender and slightly scorched. Remove from heat. When cool enough to handle, cut kernels from cobs; transfer to a medium bowl and set aside. Just before serving, add tomato and the remaining oil and remaining juice, season to taste; toss to combine.

3 Meanwhile, make crushed avocado.

4 Warm the tortillas on the barbecue for 1 minute each side, then wrap in a tea towel and set aside to steam.

5 Thread chicken pieces onto 20 bamboo skewers (see notes); cook on barbecue for 8 minutes or until browned and cooked through, turning occasionally. Serve chicken skewers with tortillas, corn salad, crushed avocado and lime wedges. Garnish with coriander sprigs.

CRUSHED AVOCADO Combine ingredients in a medium bowl; season to taste and refrigerate until required.

COOKING NOTES

For this recipe, soak the skewers in cold water for 30 minutes.

Pasilla chillies are dried Mexican chillies with a deep smoky flavour. They're available from specialty spice shops (such as Herbie's Spices) and some specialty/gourmet food stores. If unavailable, substitute smoked paprika.

RASPBERRY NOUGAT FROZEN PARFAIT

SERVES

8

PREP + COOK TIME

25 MINUTES
+ FREEZING
& REFRIGERATION

Ingredients

2 cups (400g) ricotta

¾ cup (165g) caster sugar

¼ cup (40g) whole almonds, roasted, chopped coarsely

150g nougat, chopped coarsely

300ml thickened cream

1 cup (135g) frozen raspberries

Method

1 Line the base and sides of a 14cm x 21cm loaf pan with foil or baking paper, extending 5cm over long sides.

2 Blend or process ricotta and sugar until smooth; transfer to a large bowl. Stir in nuts and nougat.

3 Beat cream in a small bowl with an electric mixer until soft peaks form. Fold cream into ricotta mixture; fold in raspberries.

4 Spoon mixture into pan, cover with foil; freeze for 3 hours or overnight until firm.

5 Before serving, place parfait in the fridge for 15 minutes to soften slightly. Turn parfait out onto a board and cut into slices.

serving suggestion Serve with a raspberry sauce: cook 2½ cups (330g) frozen raspberries with ¼ cup (55g) caster sugar in a medium saucepan, stirring, over low heat, until berries are very soft. Push the mixture through a coarse sieve into a medium bowl; discard seeds. Just before serving, stir 500g fresh raspberries into sauce.

COOKING NOTES

Before cutting the parfait into slices, dip the knife in hot water – this will make it easier to cut.

The parfait can be made and frozen up to 1 week ahead.

HONEY PANNA COTTA WITH APRICOTS IN THYME SYRUP

SERVES

8

PREP + COOK TIME

1 HOUR
+ COOLING
& REFRIGERATION

Ingredients

3 teaspoons gelatine

¼ cup (60ml) water

600ml buttermilk

½ cup (125ml) pouring cream

½ cup (175g) honey

APRICOTS IN THYME SYRUP

2 cups (500ml) water

½ cup (175g) honey

2 teaspoons thyme leaves

12 small apricots (600g), halved, seeded

1 tablespoon lemon juice

Method

1 Sprinkle gelatine over the water in a small heatproof jug; stand jug in a small saucepan of simmering water, stir until gelatine dissolves.
2 Meanwhile, bring buttermilk and cream to the boil in a medium saucepan; remove from heat. Whisk in honey and gelatine mixture; strain into a large jug. Cool.
3 Divide buttermilk mixture among 8 x ⅔-cup (160ml) glasses. Refrigerate for 6 hours or overnight until set.
4 Make apricots in thyme syrup.
5 Serve panna cotta topped with apricots in thyme syrup.

APRICOTS IN THYME SYRUP
Bring the water, honey and thyme to the boil in a medium saucepan. Add apricots; simmer gently, uncovered, for 5 minutes or until almost tender. Remove from heat; add the juice, cool. Refrigerate until cold.

FRUIT CAKE CREAM PARFAITS

SERVES

6

PREP TIME

20 MINUTES

Ingredients

250g mascarpone cheese

¼ cup (60ml) whisky

1 tablespoon icing sugar, sifted

½ cup (125ml) thickened cream, whipped

300g fruit cake, crumbled

fresh raspberries, to serve

Method

1 Combine mascarpone, 2 tablespoons of the whisky and the icing sugar in large bowl; fold in cream.

2 Sprinkle half the cake into 6 x ¾-cup (180ml) glasses; sprinkle with half the remaining whisky. Spoon in half the mascarpone mixture. Repeat layering with remaining cake, whisky and mascarpone mixture. Cover; refrigerate until required. Serve topped with raspberries.

TROUBLESHOOTING

If things don't go according to plan, take a deep breath and try to see the funny side of the situation. I've hosted many occasions where the things that went seriously wrong were the actual highlights! The golden rule is to relax and enjoy the moment as best you can. If all else fails, open another bottle and remain calm!

Slow RSVPs

If people haven't responded to your invitation and it's only a week away, call, text or send an email to confirm they're coming. If in doubt, consider additional people you can invite if your friends can't make it.

Running late

PREPARE EARLY WITH ENOUGH TIME TO FINALISE FOOD AND DECOR BEFORE GUESTS ARRIVE, BUT IF YOU'RE RUNNING LATE, SORT OUT THE DRINKS FIRST. YOU CAN WORK ON THE FOOD WHILE EVERYONE IS HAVING A DRINK. MAKE SURE YOU HAVE PARTY PANTRY ESSENTIALS ON STANDBY, LIKE NUTS, CHEESE, CRISPS AND OLIVES.

Bad day, want to cancel

YOU'RE TIRED, GOT FIRED, OR BROKE UP WITH YOUR PARTNER... I'M SORRY, BUT AS TOUGH AS THIS IS, YOU CANNOT CANCEL! MAKE THE MOST OF IT... HAVE A DRINK, FORGET ABOUT YOUR DAY AND ENJOY YOUR TIME WITH GOOD FRIENDS.

Budget blowout

The best way to avoid a budget blowout is with planning. There are plenty of inexpensive ways to host a brilliant occasion, like barbecues, "potlucks" and BYO occasions, where you do the hosting and guests can bring their favourite food and drinks.

Dinner disaster

Overcooked meal, oven doesn't work... Try to stick to recipes that are easy to prepare and that you've practised before. Have ingredients for a back-up dish ready, just in case. I like to have Chinese dumplings in the freezer, which are easy to steam. With a bottle of soy sauce in the pantry, you're set. If you get stuck, order in good home-delivered food.

RUN OUT OF DRINKS

Stock up your bar with more drinks than you think you'll need. If you run out, though, don't drink and drive. Get a taxi or nominate someone to get a cab to the local bottle shop.

Power failure

LOAD UP ON CANDLES AND MATCHES AND HAVE A TORCH HANDY. ALSO STOCK UP ON PILLAR CANDLES, SO YOU CAN EMBRACE THE GLOW OF SOFT CANDLELIGHT. THIS MAY TURN YOUR PARTY INTO SOMETHING EVEN MORE SPECIAL.

Sound system blows up

Test your sound system before your occasion. You can generally get inexpensive speakers for your iPod or iPhone most weekday nights until late, and on weekends. If you can't track any down, try tuning into a music channel on your TV. If all else fails, think outside the box... an impromptu jam session perhaps?

GATECRASHERS

If unwelcome people turn up at your door (and if you really don't want them at your place), tell them politely that this is not a good time.

GUESTS STAY TOO LATE

If you know in advance that you want to wrap up your party by a certain time, include the finish time in your invitation. On the night itself, you can give signals by cleaning up the dining table and kitchen, turning down the music and turning up the lights. If guests hang around too long, ask what they're up to the next day and mention you have an early start... that should do the trick!

Guests not getting along

You never really know how everyone is going to get along. Make sure to keep one ear on conversations to see if all guests are comfortable. If there's a personality clash, very subtly move in and draw the conversation away or ask one of your guests to give you a hand in the kitchen.

Neighbours complain

Try letting neighbours know about your occasion beforehand. If they call the police to complain about the noise, turn down the music and close the doors. Don't face off with neighbours or let your guests "sort them out". Remember... you have to face your neighbours in the light of day.

WINE SPILLS ON CARPETS

If you're precious about carpets and fabrics, Scotchgard them well beforehand. If there's a spill, pour a little soda water onto the stain and leave it for a few minutes. Then pour on a handful of bicarbonate of soda and leave for 30 minutes before vacuuming. Don't rub it with a towel or let guests "fix it up" – and be careful not to make so much of a fuss that guests feel uncomfortable. For stubborn stains, call a carpet cleaner the next day.

Conversion chart

MEASURES

One Australian metric measuring cup holds approximately 250ml; one Australian metric tablespoon holds 20ml; one Australian metric teaspoon holds 5ml.

The difference between one country's measuring cups and another's is within a two- or three-teaspoon variance, and will not affect your cooking results. North America, New Zealand and the United Kingdom use a 15ml tablespoon.

All cup and spoon measurements are level. The most accurate way of measuring dry ingredients is to weigh them. When measuring liquids, use a clear glass or plastic jug with the metric markings.

The imperial measurements used in these recipes are approximate only. Measurements for cake pans are approximate only. Using same-shaped cake pans of a similar size should not affect the outcome of your baking. We measure the inside top of the cake pan to determine sizes.

We use large eggs with an average weight of 60g.

DRY MEASURES

metric	imperial
15g	½oz
30g	1oz
60g	2oz
90g	3oz
125g	4oz (¼lb)
155g	5oz
185g	6oz
220g	7oz
250g	8oz (½lb)
280g	9oz
315g	10oz
345g	11oz
375g	12oz (¾lb)
410g	13oz
440g	14oz
470g	15oz
500g	16oz (1lb)
750g	24oz (1½lb)
1kg	32oz (2lb)

LIQUID MEASURES

metric	imperial
30ml	1 fluid oz
60ml	2 fluid oz
100ml	3 fluid oz
125ml	4 fluid oz
150ml	5 fluid oz
190ml	6 fluid oz
250ml	8 fluid oz
300ml	10 fluid oz
500ml	16 fluid oz
600ml	20 fluid oz
1000ml (1 litre)	1¾ pints

LENGTH MEASURES

metric	imperial
3mm	⅛ in
6mm	¼in
1cm	½in
2cm	¾in
2.5cm	1in
5cm	2in
6cm	2½in
8cm	3in
10cm	4in
13cm	5in
15cm	6in
18cm	7in
20cm	8in
22cm	9in
25cm	10in
28cm	11in
30cm	12in (1ft)

OVEN TEMPERATURES

The oven temperatures in this book are for conventional ovens;
if you have a fan-forced oven, decrease the temperature by 10-20 degrees.

	°C (CELSIUS)	°F (FAHRENHEIT)
Very slow	120	250
Slow	150	300
Moderately slow	160	325
Moderate	180	350
Moderately hot	200	400
Hot	220	425
Very hot	240	475

Index

Published in 2015 by
Bauer Media Books, Australia.
Bauer Media Books are published by
Bauer Media Pty Limited.

MEDIA GROUP

BAUER MEDIA BOOKS
Publisher Jo Runciman
Editorial & food director Pamela Clark
Director of sales, marketing & rights Brian Cearnes

Project manager & Operations manager
David Scotto
Creative director Hieu Chi Nguyen
Designer Jeannel Cunanan
Editor Lynette Justice
Food editor Rebecca Meli

Published by Bauer Media Books,
a division of Bauer Media Pty Limited,
54 Park St, Sydney; GPO Box 4088,
Sydney, NSW 2001, Australia.
phone +61 2 9282 8618; fax +61 2 9267 3702
www.awwcookbooks.com.au

Printed in China with 1010 Printing Asia Limited.

A catalogue record for the book is available from the
National Library of Australia

ISBN 978-1-74245-618 8 (hardback)

Bauer Media Pty Limited 2015

ABN 18 053 273 546

Cover photography Ben Dearnley
Cover styling Kristen Wilson

Additional photography Ben Dearnley,
Tanya Zouev

Additional styling Kristen Wilson
Photochef Tessa Immens

Assistant photochef Nadia Fonoff

Hair & make-up Nicole Orlich

To order books

phone 136 116 (within Australia) or order online at
www.magshop.com.au